OPPOSING
VIEWPOINTS®
SERIES

# The Catholic Church

# Other Books of Related Interest:

## At Issue Series

How Does Religion Influence Politics?

Reproductive Technologies

## Global Viewpoints

Religion

## Introducing Issues with Opposing Viewpoints Series

Gay Marriage

Women's Rights

## Issues on Trial

Birth Control

"Congress shall make no law ... abridging the freedom of speech, or of the press."

*First Amendment to the U.S. Constitution*

The basic foundation of our democracy is the First Amendment guarantee of freedom of expression. The Opposing Viewpoints Series is dedicated to the concept of this basic freedom and the idea that it is more important to practice it than to enshrine it.

SERIES

# I The Catholic Church

*Noah Berlatsky, Book Editor*

**GREENHAVEN PRESS**
*A part of Gale, Cengage Learning*

GALE
CENGAGE Learning™

Detroit • New York • San Francisco • New Haven, Conn • Waterville, Maine • London

Christine Nasso, *Publisher*
Elizabeth Des Chenes, *Managing Editor*

© 2011 Greenhaven Press, a part of Gale, Cengage Learning

*For more information, contact:*
Greenhaven Press
27500 Drake Rd.
Farmington Hills, MI 48331-3535
Or you can visit our Internet site at gale.cengage.com

For product information and technology assistance, contact us at

Gale Customer Support, 1-800-877-4253
For permission to use material from this text or product, submit all requests online at www.cengage.com/permissions

Further permissions questions can be emailed to permissionrequest@cengage.com

Articles in Greenhaven Press anthologies are often edited for length to meet page requirements. In addition, original titles of these works are changed to clearly present the main thesis and to explicitly indicate the author's opinion. Every effort is made to ensure that Greenhaven Press accurately reflects the original intent of the authors. Every effort has been made to trace the owners of copyrighted material.

Cover image courtesy of Rokusek Design, Inc. Image copyright © Alistair Cotton, 2010. Used under license from Shutterstock.com.

**LIBRARY OF CONGRESS CATALOGING-IN-PUBLICATION DATA**

The Catholic Church / Noah Berlatsky, book editor.
    p. cm. -- (Opposing viewpoints)
    Includes bibliographical references and index.
    ISBN 978-0-7377-5104-8 (hardcover) -- ISBN 978-0-7377-5105-5 (pbk.)
    1. Sex--Religious aspects--Catholic Church. 2. Catholic Church--Doctrines. 3. Church growth--Catholic Church. 4. Catholic Church--Membership. I. Berlatsky, Noah.
    BX1795.S48C37 2010
    282--dc22

                                2010012406

Printed in the United States of America
1 2 3 4 5 6 7 14 13 12 11 10

# Contents

## Chapter 3: How Should the Catholic Church Approach Reproductive and Sexual Issues?

## Chapter 4: How Can the Catholic Church Grow?

# Why Consider Opposing Viewpoints?

> *"The only way in which a human being can make some approach to knowing the whole of a subject is by hearing what can be said about it by persons of every variety of opinion and studying all modes in which it can be looked at by every character of mind. No wise man ever acquired his wisdom in any mode but this."*
>
> *John Stuart Mill*

In our media-intensive culture it is not difficult to find differing opinions. Thousands of newspapers and magazines and dozens of radio and television talk shows resound with differing points of view. The difficulty lies in deciding which opinion to agree with and which "experts" seem the most credible. The more inundated we become with differing opinions and claims, the more essential it is to hone critical reading and thinking skills to evaluate these ideas. Opposing Viewpoints books address this problem directly by presenting stimulating debates that can be used to enhance and teach these skills. The varied opinions contained in each book examine many different aspects of a single issue. While examining these conveniently edited opposing views, readers can develop critical thinking skills such as the ability to compare and contrast authors' credibility, facts, argumentation styles, use of persuasive techniques, and other stylistic tools. In short, the Opposing Viewpoints Series is an ideal way to attain the higher-level thinking and reading skills so essential in a culture of diverse and contradictory opinions.

In addition to providing a tool for critical thinking, Opposing Viewpoints books challenge readers to question their own strongly held opinions and assumptions. Most people form their opinions on the basis of upbringing, peer pressure, and personal, cultural, or professional bias. By reading carefully balanced opposing views, readers must directly confront new ideas as well as the opinions of those with whom they disagree. This is not to simplistically argue that everyone who reads opposing views will—or should—change his or her opinion. Instead, the series enhances readers' understanding of their own views by encouraging confrontation with opposing ideas. Careful examination of others' views can lead to the readers' understanding of the logical inconsistencies in their own opinions, perspective on why they hold an opinion, and the consideration of the possibility that their opinion requires further evaluation.

## Evaluating Other Opinions

To ensure that this type of examination occurs, Opposing Viewpoints books present all types of opinions. Prominent spokespeople on different sides of each issue as well as well-known professionals from many disciplines challenge the reader. An additional goal of the series is to provide a forum for other, less known, or even unpopular viewpoints. The opinion of an ordinary person who has had to make the decision to cut off life support from a terminally ill relative, for example, may be just as valuable and provide just as much insight as a medical ethicist's professional opinion. The editors have two additional purposes in including these less known views. One, the editors encourage readers to respect others' opinions—even when not enhanced by professional credibility. It is only by reading or listening to and objectively evaluating others' ideas that one can determine whether they are worthy of consideration. Two, the inclusion of such viewpoints encourages the important critical thinking skill of objectively evaluating an author's credentials and bias. This evaluation will illuminate an author's reasons for taking a particular stance on an issue and will aid in readers' evaluation of the author's ideas.

It is our hope that these books will give readers a deeper understanding of the issues debated and an appreciation of the complexity of even seemingly simple issues when good and honest people disagree. This awareness is particularly important in a democratic society such as ours in which people enter into public debate to determine the common good. Those with whom one disagrees should not be regarded as enemies but rather as people whose views deserve careful examination and may shed light on one's own.

Thomas Jefferson once said that "difference of opinion leads to inquiry, and inquiry to truth." Jefferson, a broadly educated man, argued that "if a nation expects to be ignorant and free . . . it expects what never was and never will be." As individuals and as a nation, it is imperative that we consider the opinions of others and examine them with skill and discernment. The Opposing Viewpoints Series is intended to help readers achieve this goal.

*David L. Bender and Bruno Leone,*
*Founders*

# Introduction

> *"Dear brothers and sisters, after the great Pope John Paul II, the cardinals have elected me—a simple, humble worker in the vineyard of the Lord."*
>
> *—Pope Benedict XVI,*
> *2005*

The College of Cardinals elected Cardinal Joseph Ratzinger pope in 2005 following the death of the long-serving Pope John Paul II. Ratzinger took the name Pope Benedict XVI.

Before his election as pope, Cardinal Ratzinger was already an extremely influential figure within the Catholic Church. Born in Germany in 1927, Ratzinger became a priest in 1951 and received his doctorate in theology in 1959, according to Eternal Word Television Network (EWTN). He taught theology at several European universities, gaining a reputation as a skillful and talented theologian. In 1977 Pope Paul VI elected Ratzinger archbishop of Munich. Soon thereafter, he became a cardinal.

In 1981 Ratzinger became head of the Congregation for the Doctrine of the Faith, a Vatican department that enforces theological orthodoxy. During this time, he became a close advisor to Pope John Paul II. According to an article from the Catholic News Service on April 19, 2005, "Insiders said [Ratzinger's] influence was second to none when it came to setting Church priorities and directions and responding to moral and doctrinal challenges."

As the head of the Congregation for the Doctrine of the Faith, Ratzinger was at the forefront of the Church's effort to stamp out liberation theology in the 1980s. Members of this

Latin American movement argued that the Church had a religious obligation to help its followers in the struggle against tyrannical social, economic, and political institutions. Liberation theology advocates often use the theories of political philosopher Karl Marx as a way to understand the teachings of Jesus. Ratzinger and other critics believed in helping the poor and the oppressed, but they condemned the use of political philosophies such as Marxism as a method of interpreting scripture. These criticisms effectively silenced the movement within the Church.

Ratzinger has long argued that Catholics should not dissent from the Church on essential religious matters. In line with this view, the Congregation for the Doctrine of the Faith published a document in 2003 stating that Catholic politicians should not ignore Church teachings. This raised the question of whether priests should deny Communion to Catholic politicians who support the right to abortion.

Both before and after his elevation to the papacy, Ratzinger was, and continues to be, concerned about what he sees as the problem of relativism. In his address at his inaugural mass, for example, he noted, "Today, a particularly insidious obstacle to the task of educating is the massive presence in our society and culture of that relativism which, recognizing nothing as definitive, leaves as the ultimate criterion only the self with its desires. And under the semblance of freedom, it becomes a prison for each one, for it separates people from one another, locking each person into his or her own 'ego.'"

Like other popes before him, Benedict has been involved in a number of controversies. One of the most reported incidents involved a 2006 lecture during which Benedict quoted a fourteenth-century theologian who suggested that Islam was an inherently violent religion. The pope's remarks led to protests around the globe, during which angered protesters burned several Catholic churches. Benedict apologized for using the quote and pointed out that the statement does not reflect his personal opinion. He has repeatedly reached out to Muslims since making the statement, and even visited an Islamic place of worship in Turkey. According to *New York Times* reporter Ian Fisher, Ratzinger is "only the second pope in 2,000 years known to have visited a mosque."

The pope also caused a stir during a flight to Africa in 2009 when reporters asked him to comment on the HIV/AIDS crisis. In regard to the use of condoms to combat AIDS, the pope stated that "the problem cannot be overcome by the distribution of prophylactics: on the contrary, they increase it," as quoted in the *Lancet* on May 9, 2009. The pope's statement caused a media frenzy. According to Michael Webb on the Alligator Web site, given the AIDS crisis in Africa, where 22 million people have HIV, the pope's comments "provoked strong reactions. Journalists, politicians and AIDS activists from around the world lined up to criticise the pope's views." The pope's supporters, however, contend that Benedict's statement was in line with the Catholic Church's long-standing opposition to both condoms and sex outside marriage.

Benedict's most extensive effort to address social issues came in a 2009 encyclical titled *Caritas in Veritate*, or *Charity in Truth*. The letter focuses on the problems of global development and progress, arguing that world leaders must address these issues with love and truth. For instance, Benedict warns against viewing the pursuit of human rights and development as a technological or financial process. He writes, "Often the development of peoples is considered a matter of financial engineering, the freeing up of markets, the removal of tariffs, investment in production, and institutional reforms—in other words, a purely technical matter. All these factors are of great importance, but we have to ask why technical choices made thus far have yielded rather mixed results. We need to think hard about the cause. Development will never be fully guaranteed through automatic or impersonal forces, whether they derive from the market or from international politics. Development is impossible without upright men and women, without financiers and politicians whose consciences are finely attuned to the requirements of the common good."

The controversies Pope Benedict has confronted during his tenure mirror many of the important issues the Church faces today, from discussions of faith, to struggles over morals and sexuality, to issues of global development and interfaith relations. The authors in *Opposing Viewpoints: The Catholic Church* examine some of these issues in the following chapters: Who Should Be Allowed to Become a Catholic Priest? How Should the Catholic Church Approach the Issue of Homosexuality? How Should the Catholic Church Approach Reproductive and Sexual Issues? and How Can the Catholic Church Grow? The answers to these questions may provide a better understanding of the Catholic Church's role in the twenty-first century and beyond.

# Who Should Be Allowed to Become a Catholic Priest?

# Chapter Preface

In 2002 Argentinean priest Rómulo Antonio Braschi presided over the ordination of seven women as Roman Catholic priests on a boat in Germany's Danube River. This incident caused unrest within the Catholic Church, which does not recognize the ordination of women as priests.

In response to Braschi's unsanctioned actions, the Vatican gave the women, known by the media as the Danube Seven, a month to retract their vows. When they refused, the Vatican excommunicated them, preventing the women from taking part in official Catholic rites. According to an article from the British Broadcasting Corporation (BBC) on August 5, 2002, the Vatican took this step "because the women . . . gave no indication of amendment or repentance for the most serious offence they had committed."

The Vatican had hoped that excommunication would convince the women to renounce their vows and return to the Church as laypeople. Instead, the Danube Seven ignored the Church's wishes and continued acting as priests, presiding over weddings and funerals. In 2005 members of the group presided over the informal ordination of another young woman. BBC reporter Julian Pettifer attended the ceremony. In a June 22, 2005, article, he explained that the ceremony "was primarily an act of protest" against the Church.

In the article, Pettifer also noted that most of the Catholics he spoke to at the ceremony "would welcome women into the Roman Catholic priesthood." When Pettifer presented this information to Archbishop John Paul Foley, president of the Pontifical Council for Social Communications, the priest claimed that the issue of women priests is about Church law, not "opinion polls."

Today, the schism between the Vatican and the self-declared women priests remains. On July 29, 2009, Christine

Mayr-Lumetzberger, one of the Danube Seven, spoke with Russian news organization RT. She told the reporter that she continues to perform priestly functions in her home in Austria. Mayr-Lumetzberger even set up a private chapel, where she presides over baptisms, weddings, and funerals. She explained, "I want to have change in the Roman Catholic Church and this is one of the reasons I want to stay in the Roman Catholic Church. It is like a family." Still, Church officials do not support Mayr-Lumetzberger's views. In the same report, Erich Leitenberger, a spokesperson for the Vienna Archdiocese, said, "I think that in the next hundred, 200 or 300 years we will not have women bishops or women priests inside the Roman Catholic Church." The following viewpoints further explore the struggle within the Catholic Church to determine who has the right to be ordained a priest.

> *"Yes, we know that the early Church featured married apostles, and, in the early centuries, married priests were common. But even though they were married, they were expected to be continent after their ordination."*

# Celibacy Is an Important Part of the Priesthood

## Cale Clark

*A "re-vert" to the Catholic faith, Cale Clark is a lay pastoral assistant in Unionville, Ontario, Canada. He is also the creator of FX: The Faith Explained, a seminar series on Catholic apologetics. In the following viewpoint, Clark provides some reasons for supporting celibacy in the priesthood. Clark cites the difficulties that women face as wives of pastors and the difficulties that pastors face in caring for a congregation and a spouse at the same time. Clark also finds support for a celibate priesthood in the example of Jesus and in a conversation between Peter and Jesus relating to what the apostles had given up to follow Christ.*

Cale Clark, "Priestly Celibacy: Practical Advantages and Apostolic Origins," *Catholic Insight*, December 2007. Copyright © 2007 *Catholic Insight*. Reproduced by permission.

As you read, consider the following questions:

1. According to Clark, what is the primary reason why pastors leave their ministries?

2. According to Clark, what role does Jesus play in the Church's decision to require priests to be celibate?

3. According to Clark, what is one of the biblical passages that provides evidence for the requirement of a celibate priesthood?

A recent edition of *Time* magazine featured a piece about the wives of Protestant clergy in the U.S., and how they derive mutual support via everything from conferences to Web-based communities.

It is often difficult for Catholics to appreciate the hardships these women endure. Often, their role in supporting their spouses' ministries amounts to that of an unpaid staff person to their congregation. Furthermore, they are ever cognizant that all eyes in their communities are fixed on them, as they are judged (fairly or not) on everything from their appearance to the behaviour of their children.

The *Time* article notes that "eight in ten pastors' wives feel underappreciated or unaccepted by their husbands' congregations, according to surveys by the Global Pastors Wives Network (GPWN); the same number wish their husbands would choose another profession. 'Wives' issues' is the No. 1 reason pastors leave their ministries, and the divorce rate among ministers and their wives is 50%, no better than that of the general U.S. public." One would guess that Canadian stats would be similar.

Trying to serve the Bride of Christ and your own bride, God's children as well as your own can be trying indeed. These facts are perhaps not often considered by those who feel a more widespread allowance of marriage for Catholic clergy would attract more candidates to the priesthood. Celibacy is a discipline, after all, not a dogma, and there are married Catholic priests who have been given dispensation from this law.

But more importantly than any practical considerations, does priestly celibacy claim apostolic origins?

First, Jesus himself was celibate. This fact alone deserves deep reflection when considering what the ideal lifestyle should be of those men who are called to the imitation of Christ in a special way, who act "in the person of Christ."

A common objection to priestly celibacy is this: "How can Catholics deny their priests and bishops marriage when the New Testament clearly teaches that at least some of the apostles were married? Jesus even healed Peter's mother-in-law, for Pete's sake!"

Yes, we know that the early Church featured married apostles, and, in the early centuries, married priests were common. But even though they were married, they were expected to be continent after their ordination. That is, they abstained from sexual relations when they began following Jesus in the apostolic ministry.

The New Testament itself bears witness to this. After Peter himself complained, "Behold, we have left our homes and followed you," Jesus replied: "Truly, I say to you, there is no man who has left house or wife or brothers or parents or children, for the sake of the Kingdom of God, who will not receive manifold more in this time, and in the age to come, eternal life" (Luke 18:28–30, emphasis mine).

Now, of course, Jesus did not advocate a heartless abandoning of one's wife and family. Jesus's anger over (and prohibition of) divorce bears out his concern for the welfare of married women, and for marriage itself. In the culture of Jesus's time, the apostles' wives were cared for by members of their extended family unit, while the apostles themselves left their homes to traverse Galilee with their Master. In fact,

## Sex and the Single Priest

The Mexican celebrity magazine *TVnotas* recently published 25 paparazzi photos of the Rev. Alberto Cutié, the popular Miami Beach priest famous for his Spanish-language television and radio talk shows, cavorting amorously on a Florida beach with an attractive woman. Over a three-day period, the pictures also captured him kissing her in a bar. In one of *TVnotas*'s "in fraganti" shots, the woman wraps her legs around Cutié; in another, Cutie has a hand down her swimsuit, fondling her rear end.

Because of the scandal, the Archdiocese of Miami says Cutié, 40, is no longer the administrator of his Miami Beach parish, and it has barred him from leading Sunday Mass there.

*Tim Padgett,*
*"The Father Cutié Scandal: Sex and the Single Priest,"*
Time, *May 7, 2009. www.time.com.*

the healing of Peter's mother-in-law (Mark 1:30–31) took place at his own house in Capernaum.

Many opponents of clerical celibacy will cite St. Paul's admonition that a bishop must be "married only once" (1 Tim. 3:2). But this, of course, never meant that a bishop must be married, or else he could no longer be bishop if his wife died! What this meant was that a bishop could not be married more than once in his life, or be a bigamist. Also, if a man had been married again after the death of his first wife, it would cast serious doubt on his ability to keep priestly continence should he be ordained bishop.

Space limits prevent me from citing other scriptures and early Church laws from East and West verifying the apostolic origins of priestly celibacy. But, because of these demands, the Church over time began to see the wisdom of an unmarried priesthood, and this is why even today, in the Latin Church, only those who "have renounced marriage for the sake of the kingdom of heaven" (Matt. 19:12) are normally considered for this honour.

*"The Roman Catholic Church's ban on married heterosexual priests has been, is, and will be self-destructive."*

# Celibacy Should Not Be a Requirement for Catholic Priests

*Marc Pascal*

*Marc Pascal is a lawyer, a consultant, and a writer for the Moderate Voice Web site. In the following viewpoint, he argues that the ban on married priests is illogical because the Church allowed priests to marry for more than a thousand years. Today, the Church allows a small number of priests to marry under certain circumstances. Pascal also argues that the ban on marriage is self-destructive and that it is responsible for the current shortage of priests. The author contends that allowing priests to marry might open the door to other social changes within the Catholic Church.*

As you read, consider the following questions:

1. As cited by Pascal, how long has the celibacy requirement existed in the Catholic Church?

Marc Pascal, "The Catholic Church, Priestly Celibacy, and Gay Marriage," The Moderate Voice, June 2, 2009. Reproduced by permission of the author.

2. According to Pascal, has the Catholic laity increased or decreased over the past fifty years?

3. What does Pascal suggest may be the reason for the Church's strong stance against gay marriage?

The Roman Catholic Church's ban on married heterosexual priests has been, is, and will be self-destructive. It is also without any meritorious religious basis. Most of the original 12 Jewish disciples of the Rabbi Jesus were married men. Married priests were common for over a thousand years in the Church. This celibacy requirement is only about a couple hundred years old. A number of past popes were married and at least one pope was the father of another.

## The Celibacy Requirement Is Inconsistent

Most of the world's religions find their best recruits for the next generation of spiritual leaders among the children of married rabbis, ministers, and imams. This leaves the Catholic Church with about 1 billion worldwide adherents at a considerable disadvantage.

If a married Episcopal or Anglican priest leaves that church and becomes a Catholic priest, he can stay married. The Roman Catholic Church is also in "full communion" with various Eastern sects (Ukrainian, Armenian, etc.) that permit their priests to marry.[1] The Episcopal and Anglican churches are having a major schism over women and gay priests, but there is no conflict over heterosexual married men as priests.

Father Alberto Cutié, the Roman Catholic "Latino" TV priest in Miami, fell from grace when he admitted to having fallen in love with a woman (a young boy would have been more predictable but it was a relief to many Catholics anyway). He has decided to become an Episcopalian in order to get married. In protest to the ordination of women and openly

1. Full communion means the churches share essential doctrines that unite them into a single church.

gay men as priests, some married Episcopalian priests have joined the Catholic Church and all have been allowed to stay married. With a name like Cutié, it wouldn't be a surprise if he tries to pull a stunt like that. He might be betting that it would take years for the old guys in Rome to figure that one out.

It is unlikely that the Church will be able to engage science and technology to invent a robot or hologram priest that only comes into view during the middle of mass to bless the wine and bread and then promptly disappears. It would also have to make the necessary guest appearances at weddings, funerals, and for last rites.

## Not Enough Priests

Even though the Catholic laity has grown significantly over the past 50 years, the number of priests has dropped precipitously during the same period of time. Where there were once three priests to a parish, many parishes today have to get by with only one full-time or one part-time priest who may also handle another parish or two. After the sexual scandals of the Catholic Church were exposed, many problematic priests had to retire or be assigned to administrative tasks far from parishioners and children.

The huge shortage of priests is the principal reason behind the needless closure of so many Catholic churches in the East and Midwest of the United States, and elsewhere in Canada and Europe. More than just killing off important social and charitable centers for entire neighborhoods, the Church is abandoning its flock and many important architectural and artistic treasures of U.S. urban history.

Without a minister or rabbi, most Protestant churches and Jewish congregations would flounder and die. The same holds true for Catholic communities. Every religion needs local spiritual and organizational leaders—and one in a far-off city is not going to be sufficient for the long-term growth and

## Number of Priests in Some Northeastern Dioceses, 1966, 1985, 2005

| Region and diocese | Year | | | % difference 1966–2005 |
|---|---|---|---|---|
| | 1966 | 1985 | 2005 | |
| **New England** | | | | |
| Burlington VT | 181 | 131 | 68 | −62 |
| Fall River MA | 236 | 174 | 101 | −57 |
| Hartford CT | 564 | 450 | 245 | −57 |
| Boston MA | 1,330 | 961 | 569 | −57 |
| Portland ME | 250 | 178 | 124 | −50 |
| Worcester MA | 308 | 279 | 190 | −38 |
| Norwich CT | 138 | 121 | 101 | −27 |
| **Middle Atlantic** | | | | |
| Brooklyn NY | 1,039 | 701 | 428 | −59 |
| Albany NY | 463 | 306 | 196 | −58 |
| Rochester NY | 396 | 259 | 166 | −58 |
| New York NY | 1,221 | 831 | 560 | −54 |
| Buffalo NY | 629 | 497 | 318 | −49 |
| Philadelphia PA | 1,042 | 815 | 90 | −43 |
| Newark NJ | 876 | 710 | 528 | −40 |
| Scranton PA | 467 | 372 | 285 | −39 |
| Camden NJ | 356 | 345 | 222 | −38 |
| Ogdensburg NY | 187 | 166 | 122 | −35 |
| Pittsburgh PA | 566 | 537 | 432 | −24 |
| Altoona-Johnstown PA | 159 | 165 | 123 | −23 |
| Rockville Centre NY | 449 | 418 | 358 | −20 |
| Allentown PA | 286 | 258 | 238 | −17 |

TAKEN FROM: "Priest Shortage Statistics: Northeast" *Future Church.* www.futurechurch.org.

continuity of any religious group. Even new immigrant Catholics cannot make up for the continuing losses in the Church's real membership or priesthood—and many of those immigrants also support a married priesthood. Many "lapsed" Catholics failed to find a competent priest to be their spiritual guides and they turned elsewhere for important answers.

Instead the Church has had to scramble for priests from the ever-shrinking group of men not interested in marriage. With gays eventually getting the right to marry—that group of interested men will get even smaller. It will be limited to just those men who are uninterested in having any meaningful relationships with women, men, or children—also known as "hermits." Perhaps the Church's strong stance against gay marriage is secretly fed by a fear of losing its last recruiting ground for priests.

For the majority of Roman Catholics around the world who see nothing wrong with having married heterosexual men as priests, the best route to that end may be in strongly supporting gay marriage. By ensuring that there are effectively no celibate men available for the priesthood, coupled with the glaring history of a non-celibate priesthood and current policies that permit them in associated churches, the Roman Catholic hierarchy may finally have to give in on this issue as a matter of survival.

This could be a win-win coalition between the GLBT [gay, lesbian, bisexual, and transgender] community and the Catholic laity. Proponents of Proposition 8[2] in California should present such a cogent argument to one of the largest voting blocks in the state in order to win its passage, and that would eventually have important ancillary benefits.

## A First Step Toward Change

Of course the stubborn, ossified, narrow-minded, asexual, old men in Rome may refuse any changes until they are all dead, but then that's just a short time to wait. However, the mold would have already been cast to be poured by their successors if the Church wants to be a viable religious organization in the future.

Large and old institutions change very slowly, and in light of the mess the Anglican and Episcopalian churches are in to-

2. Proposition 8 was a ballot proposition and constitutional amendment passed in 2008 in California that made gay marriage unconstitutional.

day [concerning the issue of women and homosexuals serving as priests], there probably won't be any women or openly gay people admitted to the Catholic priesthood if married hetero-sexual men can again become priests. But with so many mar-ried men (including many former priests) out there who want to be priests, the Church could be reinvigorated for genera-tions to come by taking just this small step. And over time, understanding, benevolent, and inclusive-minded heterosexual married priests with wives and children may lead to further changes in just a generation or two.

> "Men have the more active role in the relationship: The husband is the one who loves while the wife is she who is loved and in return gives love. This special capacity to receive love is what is meant by feminine submission and is the basis of the image of the submission of the Church to Christ. Submission here means to be subsequent or responsive, not necessarily obsequious or subservient."

# Women Should Not Be Priests

*Jennifer Ferrara*

*Jennifer Ferrara co-edited* The Catholic Mystique: Fourteen Women Find Fulfillment in the Church *(2004) with Patricia Sodano Ireland. Sarah Hinlicky Wilson was the Vicar of St. Paul's Lutheran Church and the Lutheran Campus Ministry at Duke University in Durham, North Carolina, at the time of writing. In the following viewpoint, which presents Ferrara's view, Ferrara explains her understanding of Pope John Paul II's view of the relationship between husband and wife and how that*

Jennifer Ferrara and Sarah Hinlicky Wilson, "Ordaining Women: Two Views (Contrasting the Views of Martin Luther and Pope John Paul II)," *First Things: A Monthly Journal of Religion and Public Life*, April 2003, pp. 33ff. Copyright © 2003 Institute on Religion and Public Life.

*relationship affects the way they can minister in the Church. Ferrara supports the view that male and female attributes are an integral part of being human. That means that men and women are not just slightly different versions of each other or of the same thing. The male is the initiator and protector while the female is the receiver and responder. The man sacrifices himself in love for the woman, and the woman responds with love in turn. This is a picture of Christ and the Church, and the priest is an icon of Christ as husband and father, a role that women cannot fulfill.*

As you read, consider the following questions:

1. According to the author's interpretation of Martin Luther, what is the cause of the differences between men and women?

2. According to this viewpoint, what precisely is a priest?

3. According to this viewpoint, why can't women be spiritual mothers or priestesses?

A decade ago, Michael Novak observed . . . that one scarcely ever encounters a theological argument against the proposition that women should be ordained priests. Though some Catholics have begun to openly defend the Church's position on women's ordination, they frequently do so with less zeal than when discussing other topics of social and cultural import. I suspect this is because orthodox Christians of every stripe are often thrown together in an "ecumenism of the trenches" and from that vantage point do not wish to dwell on subjects that divide them. Conservative Catholics who agree with the tradition of restricting the priesthood to men do not wish to offend their Protestant friends who have grown accustomed to female pastors or who may even be female pastors. Nor do they wish to insult their fellow Catholics who may think women should be ordained. A friend who is a priest explained to me that he does not openly oppose women's ordination because he knows several nuns who "suffer greatly" because they cannot be priests. It can, then, seem easiest and most charitable for those of us who oppose women's ordination to keep our opinions to ourselves.

However, in doing so, we do not help the suffering nuns, and we concede the high ground to those who wish to interpret Church doctrine in light of feminist ideology rather than the other way around. This is not a small problem: The feminists and their allies have gained ascendancy in many seminaries and dioceses throughout the country. Moreover, by way of response to the current scandals within the Church, they have ratcheted up their calls for women's ordination, despite the fact that lack of fidelity to the Church's teachings helped create the problems in the first place. . . .

## Luther's View

As a Lutheran pastor, I supported women's ordination as part of a more general argument that God did not intend men and women to have different roles, and I found support for this position in Martin Luther's writings. In his lectures on Genesis, Luther explains, "[Adam and Eve's] partnership involves not only their means but children, food, bed, and dwelling; their purposes, too, are the same. The result is that the husband differs from the wife in no other respect than sex; otherwise the woman is altogether a man." Differentiation between the sexes according to Luther is a result of the fall of our first parents: "If the woman had not been deceived by the serpent and had not sinned, she would have been the equal of Adam in all respects. For the punishment, that she is now subjected to the man, was imposed on her after sin and because of sin." As a result, she "has been deprived of the ability of administering the affairs that are outside [the home] and that concern the state."

According to Luther, the affairs outside of the home include those of the Church because the Church is an estate within the kingdom of the world and is, therefore, guided by the same laws that pertain to civil society. Galatians 3:28 ("There is neither male nor female . . . for you are all one in Christ Jesus") does not invalidate the law that subjects women to men because it applies only to the kingdom of God. According to our conscience, we are free of the law, but as long as we continue to live in an imperfect world, we are still under the law. Luther's theology of two kingdoms (law for one, gospel for the other) creates a dilemma for those theologically and confessionally orthodox Lutherans who wish to oppose women's ordination. The question they must answer is why the law subordinating women to men governs relationships in the Church and perhaps the home, but not in the rest of society. Consistency would require an across-the-board application, as Luther argued.

I believed then that this widespread inconsistency in the application of God's law invalidated calls for male headship in home and church. . . . Luther believed that the law which grants men authority over women was designed not only to punish women but also to curb evil intentions. The disciplines that derive from it serve a good purpose: "They tend to humble and hold down our nature, which could not be held in check without the cross." As a modern woman, I thought our selfish tendencies could be held in check through mutual subjection worked out through egalitarian principles. According to Luther, social arrangements should be preserved within the Church lest we give scandal to the gospel. I thought restricting ordination to men had become such a scandal; it had become a modern-day stumbling block to people's conversion and continued faith. If the subordination of women to men is, in fact, a human ordinance, we deny the principle of justification when we turn it into law. The acceptance of equality between the sexes throughout much of the world demonstrates that past generations wrongly thought the headship principle was a matter of natural law. Therefore, I thought that ordaining both men and women might well be the best way to serve our Lord in this time and place, despite 2000 years of tradition to the contrary.

## John Paul II's View

When I started to think about becoming Roman Catholic, I went back again to the beginning and read, with a critical eye, John Paul II's [*Original Unity of Man and Woman:*] *Catechesis on the Book of Genesis*. There I found an entirely different vision of creation than that set forth in Luther's lectures on Genesis. According to John Paul, Adam and Eve were not created essentially the same. Masculinity and femininity are not just attributes; rather, the function of sex is "a constituent part of the person." In other words, Eve is not Adam with a female anatomy: "Man and woman constitute two different ways of the human 'being in a body' in the unity of the image of God." Or again, "Womanhood expresses the 'human' as much as manhood does, but in a different and complementary way."

Though different, men and women both have the capacity to give of themselves and to receive love. Prior to the fall, Adam and Eve naturally gave of themselves to one another. At the time of the fall, this natural capacity for giving was lost. Henceforth, men and women are prone to view each other as objects, which is why they are now ashamed of their nakedness. Human sexuality, rather than a natural means of self-giving, becomes a way to manipulate and exploit others. Genesis 3:16 ("Your desire shall be for your husband and he shall rule over you") is not natural law, as Luther argues, but a description of the lasting consequences of original sin. In particular, the woman becomes an object of male domination. Original sin burdens the relationship between men and women, but it does not ultimately define it.

John Paul believes that radical self-giving is what, in the end, makes us human. To lord over others is the antithesis of Christian service (Luke 22:25-27) and results in a turning away from God; it is, therefore, a negation of self. Therefore, John Paul speaks of the need for mutual submission. Here he differs from other conservative Christians, including some Catholics, who think the reestablishment of responsible male headship in church and home is necessary for the reformation of church and society. The Holy Father, by contrast, says we must look to our theological pre-fall history—a history that does not involve the subordination of women to men—in order to understand the relationship to which God calls men and women. When Jesus talks about marriage, he twice uses the phrase "from the beginning." This phrase is key to John Paul's thinking about the relationship between men and women. He says Jesus asks us "to go beyond, in a certain sense, the boundary which in Genesis passes between the state of original innocence and that of sinfulness, which started with the original fall."

## The Meaning of John Paul II's Theology

When I first read these words, I was startled: They went against all my deeply ingrained Lutheran sensibilities. . . . As a Lutheran, I had thought of myself as being simul iustus et peccator (at once saint and sinner). Though Christ's righteousness had been imputed to me in exchange for my sinfulness (making me a saint), I continued to live in this world (and therefore continued to sin). Marriage was very much a part of this world. The relationship between our original parents in paradise (God's kingdom) could not be replicated in our fallen state (the kingdom of this world). For John Paul II and Catholics traditionally, the Christian life is one of progress toward holiness, the goal of which is to be like God by becoming "full of grace" (1 John 3:2).

The pope's theology of the body and of marriage can only be understood within this context. By God's grace received through the sacraments (including the sacrament of marriage), we can aspire to something greater in marriage than a power struggle hemmed in by laws designed to curb our selfish intentions. Husbands and wives can be partners in a marriage based upon a sincere and radical giving of self on the part of both spouses, a giving that results in mutual submission. Men's dominion over women is a result of the fall and is, therefore, something to be overcome in Christ, however imperfectly, in this life.

Jesus, whose authority and kingship is exercised through service, has set us free from sin and provided all people, but men in a special way, with a model for radical self-surrender and self-giving. This model is set forth in Ephesians 5:21–33 ("Be subject to one another out of reverence for Christ. Wives, be subject to your husbands, as to the Lord. . . ."). What does John Paul have to say about the portrayal of Christian marriage in what has become one of the most controversial passages in all of Scripture? He acknowledges some of the concepts in the passage are "characteristic of the mentality and customs of the times." However, he also says St. Paul demonstrates "courage" when he uses these concepts to describe how mutual subjection in Christ works. Today, our mentality and customs are different, as is the social position of women in relation to men. John Paul goes on to say, "Nevertheless, the fundamental moral principle which we find in Ephesians remains the same and produces the same results. The mutual subjection 'out of reverence for Christ' . . . always produces that profound and solid structure of the community of the spouses in which the true 'communion' of the person is constituted."

Though John Paul II never speaks of male headship, he recognizes that inherent to their natures are differences in the way men and women express love for one another. Men have the more active role in the relationship: The husband is the one who loves while the wife is she who is loved and in return gives love. This special capacity to receive love is what is meant by feminine submission and is the basis of the image of the submission of the Church to Christ. Submission here means to be subsequent or responsive, not necessarily obsequious or subservient. For the man, a love modeled upon Christ's self-sacrifice leads to a desire to provide and protect to the point of a willingness to give one's life, both literally and figuratively. Men represent Christ in a way that women cannot because men's relationship to creation is one of detachment and distance. They cannot fully share in the intimacy that women have with their children. Therefore, they better serve as an image of transcendent love, a love that is wholly other but seeks only the welfare of the other. As primarily relational beings, women are images of immanence and ultimately of the Church, which is prepared, at all times, to receive Christ's love. The result is a mutual submission, even mutual dependence, that does not undermine the role of men in church or home. . . .

At the heart of this diversity lies the difference between motherhood and fatherhood. No matter what men and women do, they bring paternal or maternal characteristics to their vocations. The Catholic saint and philosopher Edith Stein always said that all women need to accept their maternal nature if they are to accept their vocation specifically as women. This means that every woman, no matter what she does, brings maternal characteristics to her vocation. All women, married and celibate, are mothers all the time. The same can be said of men and fatherhood. John Paul reminds us that celibacy (continence for the sake of the kingdom) is not a rejection of marriage but a different form of marriage. It is a "nuptial giving of one's self for the purpose of reciprocating in a particular way the nuptial love of the Redeemer." This giving of one's self, which is the definition of conjugal love, must lead in its normal development to paternity or maternity in a spiritual sense, just as marriage does in a physical sense through procreation, rearing, and education of children.

In other words, a Roman Catholic priest is not simply a father figure; he is a father. To state what has ceased to be obvious in a society governed in large measure by the principle of androgyny, fathers and mothers are not interchangeable. Women are not men and, therefore, cannot be priests any more than they can be fathers in the physical sense. If women can step into the role of priest, then it is no longer one of fatherhood.

Why can't we have spiritual fathers (priests) and spiritual mothers (priestesses)? The answer is one that feminists do not like to hear—namely, that the priest is an icon of Christ and acts in persona Christi at the altar and in the confessional. . . . Those who favor women's ordination argue that women can represent Christ as well as men because femaleness is an attribute along the lines of Jewishness. To say that women cannot represent Christ is to suggest they are less fully human than men. This argument might have merit if it were sensible to believe that men and women are, as Luther suggests, both versions of men—and that those differences, flowing from the fall, would be overcome at the Eschaton [end of the world]. According to this line of reasoning, women should be allowed to represent Christ as a sign of the final consummation.

Such a view, however, is simply contrary to Catholic anthropology. Masculinity and femininity are not traits like skin or eye color; they are modes of being human. . . . Jesus did not just happen to be male. His masculinity is a reflection of God's paternity. God's paternity resides in His being wholly other from His creation. Of course, God is without gender and contains within Himself true masculinity and femininity. As the Catholic theologian Louis Bouyer explains in *Women in the Church*, "God is neither man nor woman, though He encompasses from the beginning all that humanity will ever bring to realization. He goes beyond masculinity in the only fatherhood worthy of the name, and is at the same time, in this eternal virginity, the antitype of all motherhood." However, the fact remains that God chose from all eternity to take the form of a man, and that Jesus is the embodiment of the Father's love.

Moreover, the priest as male represents God's transcendence. However, as symbol of the gift of Christ's love for his bride, he does not have the same sort of authority as the "rulers of the Gentiles." The priest's authority derives from service and self-sacrifice. It is an authority that should lead to mutual respect and affection between priest and parishioners, not feelings of superiority and inferiority. . . . The response of some to the current sexual crisis in the Catholic Church is to say that paternal understandings of authority need to be replaced with functional understandings. As is usually the case with those who dissent from Church teachings, they have it precisely backwards. The most obvious way to ensure fewer instances of clerical abuse in the Catholic Church would be to see that those in charge of seminaries and rectories have a clear understanding of the role of the priest as father. I am not suggesting that this is the only solution to the present crisis, but candidates for the priesthood need to be evaluated for their fitness for fatherhood. A fit father, a good father, does not abuse his children.

Instead, spiritual fatherhood has come under attack in the Church by feminists and their allies who believe the Church should reflect the unisex vision of men and women that pervades society, and they have had an influence in many dioceses and seminaries far greater than their numbers would suggest. A seminarian named Daniel Scheidt writes in the Catholic journal *Crisis* that men in seminaries and rectories are suffering from a form of identity crisis that mirrors that among men in society at large. Scheidt says that efforts to downplay the theological interrelationships of paternity (God the father) and maternity (mother Church embodied in Mary) have "taught the seminarian to be insecure and embarrassed—or even suspicious and hostile—toward facets of the

## Invalid Ordination of Women Leads to Excommunication

An invalid ordination that tried to make two women Catholic priests has spurred a strong reaction from . . . Cardinal Justin Rigali. . . .

[Rigali said,] ". . . Those who present themselves for ordination at such an invalid ceremony are, by their actions, automatically excommunicated from the Church."

*John P. Connolly,*
*"Cardinal Rigali Responds to Invalid Ordination,"*
*Bulletin (Philadelphia, PA), April 28, 2009.*
*http://thebulletin.us.*

divine mysteries that give ultimate meaning to his life as a man and, one day, as a 'Father.'" Clearly, many in the Church today are taking their cues from culture rather than traditional Catholic doctrine. . . .

Contrary to popular opinion, the Catholic Church offers a rich and multidimensional understanding of what it means for humans to be male and female, far more complex than the unisex vision of many feminists. The interplay between masculinity and femininity is by no means rigid. Catholicism has always recognized that in the spiritual life of both the married and celibate, women acquire masculine virtues and men acquire feminine ones. It is not the principle of androgyny or gender bending at work in Catholic theology. Rather, the Church has an anthropology that recognizes the differences between male and female, motherhood and fatherhood. . . .

In a tradition dating back to the early Church, all Christian souls have been described as being feminine. This is because receptivity is necessary for holiness. In the Catholic tradition, women have always provided models of holiness for men. . . . Priests are no different from other men in this regard. Unlike Jesus, they must begin by being fundamentally receptive. As [David] Schindler writes, "The ordained is first dependent upon the Marian fiat even as he is . . . empowered to represent Christ's initiative." Mary is the woman through whom the priest finds himself. What does this say about priests who steadfastly avoid having a spiritual relationship with Our Lady? If Bouyer is correct, they run the real risk of becoming profoundly and dangerously narcissistic.

Actually, everyone—male and female—suffers when Church and society no longer recognize the importance of the truly feminine or the "feminine genius," as John Paul II calls it. . . . The Catholic understanding of the feminine would be lost forever if the Church had a female priesthood. Those who insist the Church ordain women to elevate their status are, in reality, denigrating femaleness, especially motherhood. . . . We do not raise the status of women by convincing them that what they need to be is men. Though women can and should be allowed to do most of the jobs traditionally filled by men (bringing to them a feminine sensibility), they cannot and never will be biological or spiritual fathers. Those who insist otherwise effectively deny what is noble and holy about being wives and mothers (biological and spiritual) and thereby slight the importance of the feminine (mother Church) in the plan by which God intends to redeem His creation.

A loss of the feminine and its importance in the economy of salvation is part of the legacy of the Protestant Reformation and its de-emphasis of the iconic elements of faith. Luther placed the institutional Church squarely in the kingdom of the left hand, and the result was a Church more sociological in character. He also effectively denied a role for the feminine in the Church and in salvation when he developed an anthropology that took the male as the sum of what it means to be most fully human. The result was a minimalist ecclesiology that was starkly masculine in character.

For Catholics, the most important icon of the Church and the feminine is Mary, Mother of God. The diminishment of Mary and the severing of her connection to the Church by the reformers was one step along the long road to women's ordination. Interestingly, the famous Lutheran theologian Paul Tillich recognized the profound change that occurred in the Protestant churches when the figure of Mary was eliminated: "The increasingly symbolic power of the image of the Holy Virgin . . . presents Protestantism with a difficult problem. In the struggle of the Reformation against all human mediators between God and man, this symbol was abolished, and, with that process of purification, the feminine element in everything of ultimate concern was largely eliminated."

Over time, Protestantism invested God with symbols of immanence. The result has been a leveling out of the differences between creation and Creator. At the same time, the Church took on a more sociological, institutional nature. . . . These developments within Protestantism paved the way for women's ordination as ministry took on an increasingly functional nature and men no longer were seen as symbols of God's transcendence.

For those who are determined to see the Catholic Church embrace the principle of androgyny that dominates the rest of the culture, no argument against women's ordination will be persuasive. However, those who recognize the God-given inherent differences between men and women, husbands and wives, fathers and mothers, and see their importance not only for the proper working of society but for our salvation, should give thanks for the Catholic Church's resolve in adhering to two thousand years of tradition—a tradition rooted in God's good purposes for all men and women. . . .

> "The credibility of the magisterium's
> banning women from ordination bor-
> ders on zero."

# Women Should Not Be Barred from the Priesthood

## John Wijngaards

*John Wijngaards is a Catholic writer and former priest, who re-signed his ministry in protest of the Vatican's policy on women's ordination. In the following viewpoint, he argues that the ban-ning of women priests is based on secular historical Roman prac-tice, not biblical teaching. He adds that most theologians believe there is no reason to bar women from the priesthood, and he concludes by stating that he believes women will eventually gain the right to ordination.*

As you read, consider the following questions:

1. According to Wijngaards, on what grounds did Ambro-siaster say that women could not be priests?

2. According to Wijngaards, what were the most common justifications for excluding women from the priesthood in the Middle Ages?

John Wijngaards, "Women Leaders and the Catholic Church?" *Women Can Be Priests*, 2007, first published by Catholics for a Changing Church. Reproduced by permission of the author.

3. As detailed by Wijngaards, what fraction of Catholic theologians disagree with the Vatican's official position on women priests?

The Catholic Church has moved on since the day, on 29 July 1904, when Pope Pius X instructed the bishops of Italy not to trust the intelligence or reliability of women.

"In public meetings, never allow women to take the word, however respectable or pious they may seem. If on a specific occasion bishops consider it opportune to permit a meeting for women by themselves, these may not speak except under the presidency and supervision of high ecclesiastical personalities."

## Secular Gains, but Not Religious Authority

Church authorities have now come to terms with the fact that women are capable of heading academic faculties, running major corporations, ruling their countries as prime ministers or presidents. But such secular competence does not empower women to assume spiritual leadership in the Church.

Pressed on this issue during a meeting with the clergy of Rome, Pope Benedict XVI recently asserted that women contribute to the government of the Church through their manifold services. He mentioned a number of women saints of the past who have made their mark. But these services, though crucial to the Church, are purely of an auxiliary, charismatic nature, he said. The true government of the Church is reserved to men.

"The priestly ministry of the Lord, as we know, is reserved to men, since the priestly ministry is government in the deep sense, which, in short, means it is the Sacrament [of Orders] that governs the Church. This is the crucial point. It is not a particular man who does something, but the priest in him governs, faithful to his mission, in the sense that it is the Sacrament, that is, through the Sacrament it is Christ himself who governs, both through the Eucharist and in the other Sacraments, and thus Christ always presides."

The implication of this piece of typical ecclesiastical [Catholic Church] jargon is that women have no authority whatsoever in the government of the Church. Catholic belief holds that Christ entrusted authority over his Church to the apostles and their successors. This authority is threefold: the authority of teaching (imposing doctrine), the authority of consecrating (presiding at the Eucharist, performing ordinations, etc.) and the authority of ruling (imposing moral obligations, forgiving sins, taking all major decisions regarding Church discipline). Pope Benedict reiterates that all these forms of authority are imparted only by the sacrament of holy orders, which is reserved to men.

Church law puts it succinctly: "Only a baptized male validly receives sacred ordination." And: "Only those who have received sacred orders are capable of the power of governance, which exists in the Church by divine institution." In short: no Church leadership for women! You may rule a country, you'll never rule a diocese!

## Discrimination Based in Roman Law

Although present-day Church authorities attribute the ban of women from Church leadership to Jesus Christ himself ..., historical research makes clear that its origin lies in Roman law.

The influence of the Roman Empire on the organisation of the Catholic Church is undeniable. In fact, the influence has been beneficial in many respects. For the Romans were great administrators. . . .

The Romans were also good lawgivers. The great contribution of Roman legislation was its laying down of simple and clear principles. Roman law was detailed, specific, practical. . . .

But laws often hide structural prejudice, and this is what happened in the case of women. For Roman law was hostile to women. Roman family law was based on the principle that the father of the family (*pater familias*) had complete authority both over the children and his wife. This was defined as paternal power (*patria potestas*). The wife depended totally on her husband, being in fact his property. He could do with her as he liked. He could punish her in any way, even kill her, or sell her as a slave—though this last punishment was forbidden after 100 BC. And as far as family property was concerned, the wife herself did not own anything. Everything she or her children inherited belonged to her husband, including also the dowry which she brought with her to her marriage. . . .

## Assimilation into Church Discipline

If we understand that this was the condition of women *by civil law*, a law which everyone greatly respected, we can appreciate how this devaluation of women slipped into Church thinking. The inferior status of women was so much taken for granted that it determined the way Latin-speaking theologians and Church leaders would look on matters relating to women. Just listen to this reasoning by [fourth-century Christian writer] Ambrosiaster which is typical of the time:

> "Women must cover their heads because they are not the image of God. . . . How can anyone maintain that woman is the likeness of God when she is demonstrably subject to the dominion of man and has no kind of authority? For she can neither teach nor be a witness in a court nor exercise citizenship nor be a judge—then certainly not exercise leadership!"

Ambrosiaster states that woman "has no kind of authority". Why not? Because by civil law a woman could not hold any public function or exercise any authority. He goes on to say that she cannot be "a witness in court, or exercise citizenship [ = take part in public meetings] or be a judge". Why not? Because civil law forbade it. Now notice the argument. Woman does not bear the image of God *because* she is manifestly subject to man as we can see from civil law! The real argument rests on Roman law, which is taken as right and just. And here the true culprit is revealed. The cuckoo raises its ugly head. The position of woman is not really decided by any Christian tradition or inspired text, but by the pagan Roman law which was believed to be normative. . . .

## Justifications for Exclusion

The early Middle Ages saw the start of systematic theology. Thinkers began to demand reasons for everything, including for the exclusion of women from the ministries. Women were obviously substandard, they knew, but were there no exceptions? What about Mary, the mother of Jesus? Or Mary of Magdala, who had preached to the apostles? There is evidence that in the 13th century there was still room for explaining the omission of women from sacred orders as purely a Church practice, a custom that could be changed. Bonaventure (1217–1274), for instance, states: "All agree that women ought not to be promoted to Orders; but as to whether they are *capable [of Orders]*, there is doubt."

Theological ranks, however, soon closed solidly behind the Church's stand against women. A multiplicity of reasons were generated, including ridiculous ones such as that women talk too much, or that it is not becoming for them to wear the clerical tonsure. The justifications that gained most ground were these:

- Women are not created in the image of God; their purpose is to serve their husbands.

- Women still carry the curse of Eve's sin.

- Jesus Christ did not include a woman among the apostolic twelve.

- Paul forbade women to teach in church.

- Women are not perfect human beings and thus cannot represent Christ.

In recent Church documents only the last three justifications have been retained in a slightly modified form. It was Jesus Christ himself, we are told, who excluded women from the ministries for all time to come. That is why the Church has, in fact, never ordained women. Neither does the Church possess the power to change this practice. For Christ was a man, and God wants him to be represented only by men in the leadership of the Church.

This reasoning is so faulty and unsubstantiated that it would be dismissed out of hand by most present-day scholars if it were not presented in serious documents by the highest teaching authority in the Church. The Vatican's arguments, it seems to me, are as pathetic to any professional theologian as a creationist's boast that the finding of dinosaur fossils confirms the world was created 6000 years ago.

At the risk of boring my readers to tears, let me sketch the theological jousting with some cartoon-like strokes. . . .

Nowhere does Jesus Christ explicitly exclude women from leadership in his community. The fact that the first twelve apostles were only men proves nothing. The first twelve were all Jews. Does that mean only Jews can be priests? Yes but, the Vatican retorts, Jesus ordained the apostles at the last supper when he said: "Do this in commemoration of me", and only men were present. Were they? We know now that women too must have been there for the last supper was a paschal meal. Exodus 19 prescribes that women and children too had to share in a paschal meal. Moreover, whereas previously only men joined the covenant directly through circumcision, entrance into Jesus's community comes about by baptism which is the same for men and women. Paul states the consequence clearly: "Through your common baptism in Christ there is no longer any distinction between Jew and Greek, slave and free, male and female".

## Women Were Not Excluded

And what about the claim that the Church never admitted women to holy orders? It simply is not true. For at least nine centuries the Catholic Church, especially in its eastern provinces, routinely ordained women as deacons.[1] This diaconate was imparted through an ordination rite that, in today's terminology, has to be judged to be fully 'sacramental'. The bishop imposed hands on each candidate, invoking the Holy Spirit for the specific purpose of assigning the woman to the ministry of the diaconate. The ordination rites for male and female deacons were identical in all essential elements. Both men and women deacons received the diaconate stole [a garment worn by deacons]. Church legislation regulated the rights and duties of women deacons as much as that of the men. Women therefore did take part in holy orders and, according to the old principle *ex facto sequitur posse* ('from it having been done it follows it can be done'), the Church can ordain women because she has done so in the past.

Is there any validity in the rationale of Jesus Christ as a man requiring a male representative? Thomas Aquinas (1224–1274), who is quoted by the Vatican as a source for this opinion, believed women were less perfect biologically because only the male seed carried future offspring. Every woman is born incomplete, a 'monster', an 'accident of nature'. Small wonder Thomas taught that only a perfect human being, that is a male, can represent Christ.

The Vatican, while not sanctioning Aquinas's biological ignorance, yet holds on to the biological preeminence of men by seeing a significant divine symbolism in Christ's incarnation *as a man*.

"The fact that Christ is a man and not a woman is neither incidental nor unimportant in relation to the economy of salvation. . . . God's covenant with men (!) is presented in

1. A deacon is a church office or position; the office itself is referred to as a diaconate.

the Old Testament as a nuptial mystery, the definitive reality of which is Christ's sacrifice on the cross. . . . Christ is the bridegroom of the Church, whom he won for himself with his blood, and the salvation brought by him is the new covenant. By using this language, revelation shows *why the incarnation took place according to the male gender*, and makes it impossible to ignore this historical reality. For this reason, *only a man can take the part of Christ*, be a sign of his presence, in a word 'represent' him (that is, be an effective sign of his presence) in the essential acts of the covenant."

The reasoning is seriously flawed. Its derivation from prophetic imagery and Ephesians 5, 21–33 is arbitrary. It contradicts the traditional doctrine that Christ was incarnated *as a human being* (not just as a man). "The old principle states: *What is not assumed [into Christ's humanity] is not saved.* If maleness is constitutive for the incarnation and redemption, female humanity is not assumed and therefore not saved."

Also, the symbolism limps. If the Church is the bride and Christ her groom, how can the Vatican exclude women from representing the groom while including both women and men in the bride? And if Christ's maleness and the maleness of his priests is so crucial in God's plan of salvation, has the phallus not become the defining symbol of Christ in the Eucharist?

The truth of the matter is that few Catholic theologians subscribe to the official rationalizations. . . .

## Catholic Scholars See No Reason to Exclude Women

By all evidence available to me, I estimate that at least three-quarters of Catholic theologians disagree with the official position held out by the Vatican. They do not accept as proven that Jesus Christ himself excluded women from future ministries. They ascribe the woman-hostile Church practice of previous centuries to cultural bias. They see no valid reason why the Church could not admit women to all ministries and leadership positions.

"If you appoint a woman apostle, you'll have a better balanced team and avoid a lot of future bitterness and discord..."

I say: 'by all evidence available to me', for a blanket of silence has descended on the theological community after *Ordinatio Sacerdotalis*[2] (1994), which effectively forbade discussion on the question. Theologians serving seminaries and universities under Church control are, after all, required to swear

2. *Ordinatio Sacerdotalis* was a letter issued by Pope John Paul II declaring that the Church could not ordain women.

an oath of loyalty that implies agreement with the Vatican. As one theologian put to me: "I have three good reasons to keep my mouth shut. They are called Sharon, Alice and Bob—my children whom I need to feed."

With Polish rigour and German thoroughness,[3] the whole Church apparatus has been rigged to conform. The Roman Curia began consistently to fill all leadership positions with candidates favourable to its own views. Bishops are only chosen if they have first indicated that they agree with the Vatican. "Bishops are like the flagstones in St. Peter's", one Vatican source observed. "If you lay them down properly from the start, you can walk over them for the rest of their lives." It is not unlike the old Soviet Russia where all top officials had to be screened and appointed by the central politburo.

The CDF (Congregation for the Doctrine of the Faith) follows up on this structural control by censuring anyone who steps out of line. The Vatican criticises bishops in person if they have organisations in their jurisdiction that favour women priests. The Vatican sends letters to bishops ordering them to reprimand and punish Church personnel who support women's ordination, often mentioning dissident persons by name. The party line is clearly spelled out.

> "The bishop should prove his pastoral ability and leadership qualities by resolutely refusing any support to those people— whether individuals or groups—who defend the priestly ordination of women, whether they do so in the name of progress, of human rights, compassion or for whatever reason it may be."

All such repression of open discussion happens in flagrant contradiction to the solemn stipulation of the Second Vatican

3. Pope John Paul II was Polish; his successor, Joseph Ratzinger, now Pope Benedict XVI, is German.

Council[4] that "all the faithful, both clerical and lay, should be accorded a lawful freedom of inquiry, freedom of thought and freedom of expression."

As a result of Vatican pressure, most Roman Catholic theologians do not publicly discuss the issue. But I know what they think from private correspondence and from personal contacts. I am a member of the Catholic Theological Association of Great Britain, the Catholic Theological Association of Europe and the Catholic Theological Society of America. The credibility of the magisterium's banning women from ordination borders on zero. . . .

## The Church Must Change

The Catholic Church needs to shed unnecessary past accretions, such as the bias against women, and adapt itself to the new world in which we find ourselves, as the Church has done during other crucial periods in its history. Evangelisation means continuous incarnation, in which the Word can only become new flesh by taking that flesh seriously.

Will women be ordained leaders in the Catholic Church?

I look at history. The ruthless migrating nations that ravished the Roman Empire destroyed Christian communities. They also laid the foundation of flourishing Christian medieval societies. I see that atrocious horror, the Second World War, paradoxically giving birth to computers, travel by jet, nuclear energy and satellite communication. It also liberated women in many countries and brought the United Nations closer together. I see communism, contrary to everyone's calculations, crumbling in Eastern Europe even though it seemed secure under a canopy of terror.

Yes, women will become leaders in the Catholic Church: deacons, priests, bishops, and popes. Perhaps sooner than we

---

4. Second Ecumenical Council of the Vatican, or Vatican II, was a Church council held between 1962 and 1965. It liberalized or modernized a number of Church doctrines and practices.

dare expect. Christ's Spirit has not died. She is very active in the body of the Church. Though she works through human instruments, she will not fail.

*"The document cited the Church's teachings that homosexual acts are gravely sinful and that homosexual tendencies are 'objectively disordered.'"*

# Gays Should Be Barred from the Priesthood

## John Thavis

*John Thavis is a leading reporter on Catholic news at the Vatican. In the following viewpoint, he reports on a Vatican document that bars from the priesthood men with deep-seated homosexual tendencies. The document argues that homosexuality is a sin and that homosexuals are disordered and unfit to be priests. The document further adds that those who had had only transitory homosexual encounters or inclinations might still be confirmed as priests.*

As you read, consider the following questions:

1. According to Thavis, the instruction on homosexuality was published after how many years of discussion and debate?

2. How does this instruction affect already ordained priests with homosexual tendencies, as outlined by Thavis?

John Thavis, "Vatican Says No Ordaining Homosexuals, Men Who Support 'Gay Culture,'" Catholic News Service, November 29, 2005. Reproduced by permission.

3. According to Cardinal Grocholewski, what might transitory homosexual problems include?

A long-awaited Vatican document said the [Catholic] Church cannot allow priestly ordination of men who are active homosexuals, who have "deep-seated" homosexual tendencies or who support the "gay culture."

## Gay Priests Present a Risk of Negative Consequences

Such people have serious problems relating properly to men and women and present a risk of "negative consequences" that should not be underestimated, the document said.

The Vatican published the nine-page instruction from the Congregation for Catholic Education Nov. 29 [2005] after more than eight years of internal discussion and debate.

The document did not define what it meant by "deep-seated" homosexual tendencies, but contrasted them with the "transitory" problems of adolescence.

Such transitory tendencies must be clearly overcome at least three years before ordination as a deacon, it said. It did not explain what was meant by "overcome" or how that could be determined.

The document was leaked to the Italian press earlier in November.

In the United States, Bishop William S. Skylstad of Spokane, Wash., president of the U.S. Conference of Catholic Bishops, said in a statement Nov. 29 that the instruction showed a "Christian realism" about what is expected in candidates for the priesthood when it comes to their "affective maturity."

Bishop Skylstad urged bishops and major superiors to have a "prayerful and honest" discussion of the new norms with their priests and seminarians. He also made a point underlined by several other bishops: that many homosexually inclined men are, in fact, good priests.

The Vatican document was signed by Cardinal Zenon Grocholewski, prefect of the education congregation, which prepared the instruction for use by bishops, religious superiors and seminary rectors around the world.

The instruction, dated Nov. 4, was approved Aug. 31 by Pope Benedict XVI, but not in "forma specifica." That means the document carries the authority of the education congregation and does not have precedence over the existing Code of Canon Law, an informed Vatican source said.

## Objectively Disordered

In a letter accompanying the document, the Vatican made it clear that the instruction does not challenge the validity of previous ordinations of priests with homosexual tendencies, Vatican sources said.

The Vatican also communicated to bishops and seminary officials that homosexuals are not to be appointed as rectors or educators in seminaries.

"This is a logical consequence of the instruction, that those involved in formation of seminarians should have a personal situation in conformity with the norms," a Vatican official told Catholic News Service.

The document cited the Church's teachings that homosexual acts are gravely sinful and that homosexual tendencies are "objectively disordered."

In the light of those teachings, it said, the Church, while deeply respecting homosexuals, "cannot admit to the seminary or to holy orders those who practice homosexuality, present deep-seated homosexual tendencies or support the so-called 'gay culture.'"

"One must in no way overlook the negative consequences that can derive from the ordination of persons with deep-seated homosexual tendencies," it said.

"Different, however, would be the case in which one were dealing with homosexual tendencies that were only the expression of a transitory problem—for example, that of an adolescence not yet superseded," it said.

"Nevertheless, such tendencies must be clearly overcome at least three years before ordination to the diaconate," it said. Ordination as a deacon precedes priestly ordination by at least six months.

In an interview with Vatican Radio Nov. 29, Cardinal Grocholewski said "transitory" homosexual problems might include episodes of youthful curiosity, accidental acts related to a state of drunkenness, behavior by someone in prison for many years, or acts committed in order to "please someone in order to obtain favors."

"In such cases, these acts do not originate from a deep-seated tendency but from other transitory circumstances," he said.

## Superiors Must Judge Candidates

The instruction emphasized that the final judgment on ordination of candidates for the priesthood fell to bishops and to major superiors of religious orders. The bishop or major superior must arrive at a "morally certain judgment" on the candidate's qualities, it said.

"In the case of a serious doubt in this regard, he must not admit him to ordination," it said.

The document also said seminary spiritual directors have an important task in discerning the suitability of priesthood candidates. While respecting their relationship of confidentiality with seminarians, they should seek to convince those with "disturbances of a sexual nature" to abandon a priestly vocation, it said.

"If a candidate practices homosexuality or presents deep-seated homosexual tendencies, his spiritual director, as well as

# Percentage of Homosexual Priests

What percentage of priests have a homosexual orientation?

Nobody knows, with any degree of accuracy.

Any discussion of the role of homosexual orientation in the priesthood . . . is hampered by a lack of hard, reliable data.

Some estimates of the percentage of current priests with a homosexual orientation:

- According to Amanda Ripley of *Time* magazine, estimates range from 15% to 50%.

- According to Bill Blakemore of ABC News, ". . . nobody knows what percentage of the American priesthood is gay; estimates range from less than 10% to more than 30%."

- Richard Sipe, a psychotherapist and former priest, has studied celibacy, chastity, and sexuality in the priesthood for four decades. He has authored three books on the topic. He once estimated that 30% of the priesthood is homosexually oriented. Elsewhere, he is quoted as estimating that between 25% and 45% of American priests are homosexual in orientation. . . .

- Sister Maryanne Walsh, spokesperson for the national [U.S.] Conference of Catholic Bishops, said that it would be difficult to find evidence to support these [Sipe's] estimates of the percentage of gay men in the priesthood.

*B.A. Robinson, "Homosexual Orientation Among Roman Catholic Priests," ReligiousTolerance.org, November 12, 2009. www.religioustolerance.org.*

his confessor, have the duty to dissuade him in conscience from proceeding toward ordination," it said.

The document said the candidate himself also has a primary responsibility for his own formation. It would be "gravely dishonest" for a seminarian to hide his homosexuality in order to reach ordination, it said.

The text urged bishops, bishops' conferences and seminary officials to make sure that the norms are faithfully observed "for the good of the candidates themselves and to guarantee that the Church always has suitable priests who are true shepherds according to the heart of Christ."

The document said the need to issue specific norms on admitting homosexuals was "made more urgent by the current situation"; it did not elaborate on that statement.[1]

The full title of the document was *Instruction Concerning the Criteria for the Discernment of Vocations with Regard to Persons with Homosexual Tendencies in View of Their Admission to the Seminary and to Holy Orders.*

---

1. The "current situation," as of 2005, was probably the revelations of sexual abuse of boys by a number of priests.

> "Some gay priests are liberal and others are conservative. Some are still conflicted in their sexuality and others are not. What they all share is an almost heroic sense of integrity."

# Gays Should Not Be Barred from the Priesthood

## Michael Sean Winters

*Michael Sean Winters writes about religious issues for numerous publications. He is also the author of the book* Left at the Altar: How the Democrats Lost the Catholics and How the Catholics Can Save the Democrats. *In the following viewpoint, he contends that many effective and hardworking Catholic priests are gay. He argues that the Church's sexual abuse scandal is the result of secrecy and careerism—it has nothing to do with homosexual priests. Winters believes that it is wrong to exclude otherwise exemplary priests from the seminary because of their sexuality.*

As you read, consider the following questions:

1. According to Winters, what is the Church's policy on gay seminarians?

Michael Sean Winters, "Anti-Gay Auto-Da-Fé," *Slate.com*, September 28, 2005. Reproduced by permission.

2. According to Winters, what in Pope John Paul II's background led him to oppose anti-gay witch hunts?

3. According to Winters, what should the Church do in regard to the promotion of bishops in order to prevent careerism?

Last year [2004], I stumbled upon the Web site of a Catholic parish church, the pastor of which has been a friend of mine since we were in seminary together in the 1980s. Among the sermons on the site was one dealing with the sexual abuse scandal that roiled the Church in 2002. In this sermon, the priest repeated the conservative line that the scandal was largely the result of homosexual men failing to keep their vows. This did not surprise me because I knew my friend was conservative.

But I also knew he was gay. I was undisturbed because I have long believed that the accident of being gay should not prevent someone from holding whatever ideological inclinations they find compatible with the complex yearnings of their minds and hearts. I considered my friend's analysis facile and wrong, but not offensive per se until he used the pronoun "they" to describe gay men. It was with genuine concern and in a spirit of fraternal correction that I wrote my friend a note calling his attention to the fact that in English, when referring to a group of which one is a part, "we" is the proper pronoun.

## Shift in Policy

I thought of this exchange last week, as news reports filled the airwaves that the Vatican was about to ban gay priests, and my e-mail in-box and answering machine were jammed with messages of alarm, anger, and frustration. Not all messages came from gay priests; all asked me to join them in calling or writing to anyone who might be able to prevent this disaster, which I happily did. News of the purported ban seems to have been spread by right-wing gossips in the Church who were trying to advance a document on seminary practices that has been in the drafting stages for years. According to the *New York Times*, the document would declare that gay men are unfit for orders and should not be permitted to enter seminary. Pope Benedict has not yet signed the document, but anonymous Church officials quoted by the *Times* say the Vatican will soon finalize it. Church conservatives assert that the ban would represent no real shift because—they claim—barring gays from seminaries has long been Church policy. In practice, the American church has been receptive to chaste, gay seminarians.

Benedict's allies have been pushing such a ban for years. Some claimed that the document was in the final stages when John Paul II's health went into steep decline last spring.[1] But John Paul II never permitted anti-gay witch hunts. The Communists had used such tactics to smear clerics it did not like, and John Paul never permitted similar whispering campaigns to prosper.[2] Since the election of Benedict, the right-wingers in the Church have been clamoring for this document. In addition to restricting the priesthood to their own, they want to use it to help lay the entire blame for the sexual abuse crisis on homosexual priests.[3]

## Secrecy, Not Homosexuality, Is the Danger

The problem with such a ban is twofold. First, banning gay seminarians will only drive the issue underground, precisely the situation before the sexual revolution permitted people— even priests—to be more honest about their sexuality. The most notorious clerical child molesters were all ordained before the sexual revolution and before the changes wrought in

1. Pope John Paul II died in 2005. His successor is Pope Benedict XVI.
2. Pope John Paul II lived in Poland during the 1950s when the country's Communist government persecuted Catholics.
3. Since 2001, dozens of Catholic priests have been accused and/or convicted of sexually abusing minors.

## A Catholic Priest Comes Out to Support Gay Marriage

The [Reverend] Geoffrey Farrow, a Fresno [California] priest, used the pulpit Sunday to speak out against the Catholic Church's support of Proposition 8, the California ballot measure that would amend the state constitution to forbid gay marriage.

"Farrow said during the Mass that parishioners had asked him for direction and advice about [Proposition] 8. He said he came to the realization that he had to go against the Church," the *[Fresno] Bee* reported. "Before the Mass, he also told [local TV station] Channel 30 that he is gay."

Brad A. Greenberg,
"Catholic Priest Comes Out, Supports Gay Marriage,"
God Blog, October 8, 2008. www.jewishjournal.com.

the Church by the Second Vatican Council (1962–1965).[4] Secrecy and silence encourage immaturity and duplicity, necessary precursors for inappropriate sexual behavior. Second, as my exchange with my friend indicates, many of those priests the right wing considers "their own" are also gay, and only a willful ignorance would fail to see it.

Such a willful ignorance must exist. When I was in the seminary in the mid-1980s, a local bishop came to visit. The bishop dressed for Mass in the rectory next door. We seminarians were a bit late in arriving and were met by the bishop's secretary who said, "Come on boys, get into your dresses. Grandma is coming." Grandma was the bishop. The secretary had a feminine nickname, which, I am told, his intimates still

---

4. The Second Ecumenical Council of the Vatican, or Vatican II, liberalized or modernized a number of Church doctrines and practices.

use. To complete the screenplay quality of the experience, one of the priests who was in attendance that day left the priesthood shortly thereafter to become a flight steward or, as he called it, "a waitress in the sky." This kind of campiness was common both in the seminary and in my experiences with those already ordained. As for the secretary, he is now a bishop much in favor with conservatives.

The anger about the ban among priests, gay and straight, was more visceral than anything I have ever seen. It is an unwritten rule of gay life that you never, ever "out" a closeted gay person. Everyone has the right to come to terms with their own sexuality in their own way. (I need hardly add that Christians take their name from the master who famously warned against judging others.) Yet, there were threats of outings last week. The hypocrisy of trying to hang the sexual abuse crisis around the neck of gay priests, most of whom are celibate and hardworking, was too much. I know some gay priests who have truly wrestled with their sexuality. As with straight priests, some have fallen from their vows on occasion or on holiday, but most have been largely faithful. Some gay priests are liberal and others are conservative. Some are still conflicted by their sexuality and others are not. What they all share is an almost heroic sense of integrity. To try and blame them for the shiftless careerism that caused bishops to look the other way while children were being abused is beyond the pale. . . .

## End Careerism

Reform of the Church must always draw upon our tradition, and if Pope Benedict wants to truly address the source of the sexual abuse scandal, he will reinstate the ancient tradition of the Church that prevented bishops from being transferred (the technical term is "translated") or promoted from one bishopric to another, more important, diocese. In a stroke, he would remove the careerism that fueled the sweep-it-under-the-rug-at-all-costs syndrome that fostered the crisis. If a man wants to be the bishop of Bridgeport, let him be the bishop of Bridgeport for the rest of his life. But do not tempt him to fail to face problems in the hopes of becoming the archbishop of New York. This would be a useful first step.

I hope my e-mails (and this [viewpoint]) help persuade the powers that be in the Church to back off. When I approach my death, I want a kind priest at hand, and I frankly don't care what his sexual preference is. I suspect that most Catholics feel that way. It is a thing that the right-wingers hate to admit, but the Christian gospels do not suggest a culture war. They suggest that we be on the lookout for hypocrisy, especially our own.

# Periodical Bibliography

*The following articles have been selected to supplement the diverse views presented in this chapter.*

Lloyd de Vries — "Church May Ban Gay Priests," CBS News, November 5, 2002. www.cbsnews.com.

Laurie Goodstein — "A Mother, a Sick Song, and His Father, the Priest," *New York Times*, October 15, 2009.

Brad A. Greenberg — "Time to Rethink Celibacy in Catholic Church? Jesuit Publication Says So," God Blog, April 30, 2009. www.jewishjournal.com.

Brendan McDaid — "Celibacy 'Fundamental' to Priesthood, Say Bishops," *Belfast Telegraph*, November 21, 2009. www.belfasttelegraph.co.uk.

Michael Paulson — "3 Women to Be Ordained Catholic Priests in Boston," *Boston Globe*, July 18, 2008. www.boston.com.

*Religion & Ethics Newsweekly* — "Celibacy in the Priesthood," April 12, 2002. www.pbs.org.

Janice Sevre-Duszynska — "Women Priests Will No Longer Be Contained," Cincinatti.com, January 4, 2010. http://news.cincinnati.com.

William Wan — "Web Site to Out Priests Who Are Gay but Anti-Gay," On Faith, December 5, 2009. www.washingtonpost.com.

Rachel Zoll — "Priestly Struggles with Celibacy; Sex Abuse Scandal Renews Debate over Roman Catholic Ban on Married Clergy," *Washington Post*, August 31, 2003.

OPPOSING
VIEWPOINTS®
SERIES

CHAPTER 2

# How Should the Catholic Church Approach the Issue of Homosexuality?

# Chapter Preface

Gay rights, especially same-sex marriage laws, are a controversial issue in the United States. The Catholic Church opposes gay rights in general, and gay marriage in particular.

In response to the Catholic Church's opposition to gay marriage rights, activist Phil Attey developed a controversial strategy. Attey created the Web site churchouting.org (now defunct), as a way to out, or reveal the identities of, secretly gay priests in Washington, D.C. Attey said he was interested only in outing gay priests who had spoken against same-sex marriage. He refused to target priests who were in the closet (that is, whose gay identity was not public), but who did not speak against gay marriage. On the Web site, Attey explained the rationale behind the outing:

> "This site was created to provide you with the opportunity to save LGBT [lesbian, gay, bisexual, and transgender] youth from the hypocrisy of priests in the Archdiocese of Washington who are socially, romantically or sexually active gay men, yet stand silent while Archbishop [Donald] Wuerl and the U.S. Conference of Catholic Bishops increase their dogmatic war against gay families."

Many people were disturbed by the effort to out gay priests. In a post dated November 20, 2009, the author of the blog sufferthearrows.blogspot.com responded to Attey's Web site by noting that priests have little ability to influence Church policy. The author also pointed out that the situation for gay priests had deteriorated in recent years; the Church's strict policies on homosexuality have forced many gay priests back into the closet. The author explained that gay priests were "in the fulcrum of a pincer movement" between gay rights advocates and the hierarchy, and he concluded that "attacking gay priests makes as much sense as attacking gay members of the military."

The authors of the Web site Queerty also questioned Attey's strategy. In the article "If We Out D.C.'s Gay Catholic Priests, Will the Church Stop Railing Against Marriage?" the authors point out that Church leaders are unlikely to change their position on homosexuality in response to Attey's Web site. The authors also noted that Attey was not actually planning to out all gay priests. In fact, he promised to contact priests with evidence of their sexuality and give them a chance to reverse their stance on gay marriage before posting their names on his Web site. Queerty's authors referred to this policy as "sexuality blackmail."

The archdiocese responsible for Washington, D.C., expressed concern about Attey's Web site as well. Spokesperson Susan Gibbs noted that the archdiocese hoped that parishioners would contact Church authorities if they knew of a priest who was violating his vows of celibacy. However, in a December 5, 2009, entry posted on the blog On Faith, Gibbs was quoted by author William Wan as saying, "It's too easy on the Internet to gossip and violate someone's good name on rumors."

This controversy touches on many of the major issues surrounding homosexuality and the Catholic Church: the position of gay priests, the question of gay marriage, and tensions between laypeople, priests, and the hierarchy. The following viewpoints discuss each of these issues in greater detail.

"We are told that sacred scripture presents homosexual acts as acts of grave
depravity. . . . The truth about homosexuals is that they are human persons
created in the image and likeness of
God. . . . The Catechism of the Catholic Church tells us that men and
women who have homosexual tendencies are to be accepted with 'respect,
compassion, and sensitivity.'"

# The Catholic Church Rejects Homosexual Acts, but Condemns Prejudice Against Homosexual Persons

*Vincent Foy*

*Vincent Foy is a retired priest of the archdiocese of Toronto. In the following viewpoint, he contends that scripture, tradition, and reason argue against allowing marriage between homosexuals. However, he also presents the view that Christ died for homosexuals as well as for others and that Christians should treat homosexuals with respect and help them to live in chastity and virtue.*

As you read, consider the following questions:

1. What are some biblical verses that Foy uses to support his argument against homosexual marriage?

2. According to Foy, what are some reasons apart from biblical teaching to oppose homosexual marriage and homosexual acts?

3. According to Foy, what is not included in showing respect, compassion, and sensitivity to homosexuals?

Like the proverbial frog, which allowed itself to be boiled to death in a pot because the heat was turned up only gradually, society is in mortal danger because of graduated attacks on the family.

The family frog has been sitting in a warming pan for a long time. Its health and very life are threatened by no-fault divorce, contraception, sterilization, infidelity, abortion, and other societal evils like pornography and vulgarity. In Canada, the latest threat to the family is the campaign to redefine marriage so that it includes the cohabitation of homosexuals.

## The Attack

The attack on the family through the call for homosexual "unions" comes principally from the media, some judges, some politicians, some city councillors, and some homosexual groups.

In Ontario, three justices of the Superior Court of Justice, unanimously ruled, in a Divisional Court decision released July 17, 2002, that the current legal definition of marriage as a union between a man and a woman is discriminatory, and ordered it be changed to include recognition of same-sex "marriage." The court said that denying gay couples the option of marriage is unconstitutional and a violation of the Canadian Charter of Rights and Freedoms. The ruling was suspended for two years to give governments time to revise the definition of the term "marriage." Ontario Premier Ernie Eves answered that Ontario would not appeal; that is, it accepts the decree of the Ontario judges as final.

In the *Toronto Star* for August 4, 2002, there is an article with the headline: "Recognize same-sex marriages, Rock urges." We read that Canada's Health Minister, Allan Rock, a nominal Catholic, says he will work with the government to push for the recognition of same-sex marriage. In Vancouver to attend the city's Gay Pride Parade on August 4, 2002, Foreign Affairs Minister Bill Graham said that "allowing homosexuals to marry would strengthen the institution of marriage." The call for the "right" of homosexuals to marry has been supported by M.P. Svend Robinson, federal Heritage Minister Sheila Copps, and Amateur Sport Minister Paul DeVillers.

The ultimate outcome is uncertain. Federal Justice Minister Martin Cauchon said on July 29, 2002, that the federal government will appeal the decree of the Ontario Supreme Court. On August 1, 2002, Toronto city councillors voted overwhelmingly to request Martin Cauchon to abandon the federal appeal. On September 6, Justice Louise Lemelin, Quebec Superior Court judge, echoed the Ontario decision by declaring that the opposite-sex definition of marriage is discriminatory and unjustified under the Charter of Rights and Freedoms. Prime Minister [Jean] Chrétien has said that a parliamentary committee will hold national hearings and study the way other jurisdictions are handling the issue.

The latest development, as of this writing, is that in a report from LifeSiteNews.com dated September 17, we read, "In a written appeal to the Ontario Court of Appeals; the federal justice department has argued in favour of retaining the traditional definition of marriage as exclusive to heterosexuals."

## The Truth

In the present attack on family values it would be hoped that politicians, judges, homosexuals, and others would want the outcome to be based on truth: the truth about marriage, the truth about homosexuality, and the truth about homosexuals.

Is it true that homosexuals can marry? Justice Ian Pitfield of the B.C. [British Columbia] Supreme Court ruled in October 2000 that any change in the definition of marriage requires a constitutional amendment because the definition of marriage, rooted in the common law, precedes the constitution. This reasoning is legally correct but profoundly inadequate. Marriage precedes common law.

Sadly, truth is often at the mercy of whim and wish. The first temptation, directed to our first parents by Satan, was to disregard a command of God because "You will be like gods who know what is good and what is evil" (Genesis 3:5). Now judges act as though they were gods. Some legislators who supported the June 1999 parliamentary motion upholding the traditional definition of marriage now call for rejection of that motion. Are they gods who can change the nature of marriage from one year to the next? So we must ask in this matter the question which Pilate put to Christ: "What is truth?"

## The Truth About Marriage

The first relevant truth about marriage is that it was instituted by God our Creator. God, not man, determined its essential nature. Man would need to be God to change it. There is a treasure of truth about marriage in the apostolic exhortation of Pope John Paul II entitled *Familiaris Consortio*, on the role of the Christian family in the modern world (November 22, 1981). Again and again we are told that marriage is of divine origin. The document quotes Vatican Council II: "Since the Creator of all things has established the conjugal partnership as the beginning and basis of human society," the family is "the first and vital cell of society."

The second relevant truth about marriage is that it is not only a divine institution but a union of a man and woman, ordained by its nature to the continuation of the human race. Christ put it this way: "Have you not read that He who made them from the beginning made them male and female, and said, 'For this reason a man shall leave his father and mother and be joined to his wife, so the two shall become one'? So they are no longer two but one. What therefore God has joined together, let no man put asunder" (Matthew 19: 4–6).

So the truth is that marriage is of divine origin and between a man and a woman. There is not only the witness of Revelation but the witness of the major religions, of countless generations and societies. There is also the witness of reason, of the complementary nature of man and woman, and the non-complementary nature of man and man and woman and woman. Revelation, tradition, and reason instruct us about the truth of marriage.

## The Truth About Homosexuality

A compendium of the truth about homosexuality is given to us in the *Catechism of the Catholic Church*. We are told that sacred scripture presents homosexual acts as acts of grave depravity, that tradition has always declared that homosexual acts are gravely disordered and that they are contrary to natural law.

For those who wish to explore the scriptural teaching on homosexuality, the following are the principal texts: Genesis 19:14–21; Leviticus 18:22; 20:13; Romans 1:26, 27; 1 Corinthians 6:9, 10; 1 Timothy 1:9, 10. Nowhere is homosexual behaviour presented as good or praiseworthy. It is consistently presented as a grave moral evil, worthy of death and hell. It should be sufficient here to quote one passage, taken from the letter of St. Paul to the Romans (1:26, 27): "For this reason God gave them up to dishonourable passions. Their women exchanged natural relations for unnatural, and the men likewise gave up natural relations with women and were consumed with passion for one another, men committing shameless acts with men and receiving in their own persons the due penalty for their error."

Christian tradition confirms the evil of homosexual practice. It was consistently affirmed by the Fathers of the Church. Sodomy was considered one of those frightful sins which cry to heaven for vengeance, according to the ancient adage: "Clamat ad coelum vox sanguinis et sodomorum, vox oppresso rum, merces detenta laborum." This may be freely translated: "The voice of blood (murder) and of sodomy, of the oppressed, and of those labourers defrauded of their wages cry out to heaven." Sodomy was considered the blood brother of murder. Both crimes were directed against the preservation of the human race. As the Protestant theologian Roger Shinn observes: "The Christian tradition over the centuries has affirmed the heterosexual, monogamous, faithful marital union as normative for the divinely given meaning of the intimate sexual relationship."

Nor was the evaluation of homosexual practice as a grave moral evil found only in the Judaeo-Christian tradition. All major religions and societies until this age have condemned it.

There remains the argument from reason. Human anatomy proclaims sodomy unnatural. The complementarity of man and woman, physically, psychologically, and emotionally, declares it. The very body cries out against it, for disease is much more readily contracted through sodomy than through natural relations.

In sum, the argument against the evil of homosexual acts is based on revelation, tradition, and reason.

## Homosexuals Are Human Persons

The truth about homosexuals is that they are human persons created in the image and likeness of God. For them Christ died. To them, as to every human person, are addressed the words of St. Paul: "You are not called to immorality but to holiness." Right pastoral care is always in accordance with the truth. Combining the truth about marriage and homosexuality, we must conclude that homosexuals are not called to homosexual "marriage" but to live lives of chastity and love of God and others, as are we all.

The *Catechism of the Catholic Church* tells us that men and women who have homosexual tendencies are to be accepted with "respect, compassion, and sensitivity. Every sign of unjust discrimination in their regard should be avoided."

- We treat homosexuals with respect when we treat them as human persons with all the rights and obligations of human persons.

- We treat them with compassion when we encourage them to live their lives in accordance with their noble calling to chastity and virtue.

- We treat homosexuals with sensitivity when we show goodwill towards them, when we condemn all violence against them, when we avoid all derogatory remarks and labels, when we support them in all that is right and just, when we regard them as brothers and sisters in Christ.

On the contrary, we do not show "respect, compassion and sensitivity" towards homosexuals when we support laws that reward homosexual behaviour, or applaud the vulgarity and even obscenity of "gay rights" parades, when we cooperate in imprisoning them in sterile, depraved and spiritually dead unions which call lust love. An excellent document on this matter is entitled "And the Truth Will Make You Free, a Letter to Bishops of the Catholic Church on the Pastoral Care of Homosexual Persons" (Congregation for the Doctrine of the Faith, October 1, 1986).

## Consequences

Grave evils have grave consequences.

- When a society attacks the very foundation on which it is built, the nuclear family, one can predict with certainly the decline and fall of that society.

- Homosexual "marriage" would further demean fatherhood and motherhood and place an additional financial strain on parents raising a family.

- Homosexual unions are notoriously unstable despite the exceptions. The "marriage" of homosexuals would lead to an increase in divorce and litigation with accompanying financial and psychological problems.

- Homosexual "marriages" would not be the end of the deformation of marriage. It is certain that there would be pressure for the legalization of more bizarre unions. Mark Lowery, professor of moral theology at the University of Dallas, says: "If society were to give marriage benefits to homosexual persons then it could have to give the same benefits to any set of friends who so desired them."

- Homosexual "marriage" would result in a further deterioration of sex education in schools. Children would be taught that homosexuality is as normal as heterosexuality. They would be more easily seduced into homosexual experimentation. Children reared by homosexuals have their own set of problems, including the absence of a mother or father.

- Most clergymen licensed to witness marriages would refuse to assist at homosexual "marriages." This would result in a new conglomerate of confrontations. It would be more difficult to uphold the essential distinction between sin and sinner. Condemning homosexual behaviour would be more likely interpreted as a form of "homophobia."

- Above all else is the spiritual havoc which homosexual "marriage" would bring upon society in general and homosexuals in particular. There would inevitably be a lessening of already low standards of morality and a further loss of the sense of sin.

- Homosexuals themselves would be victims. Caged in a legal prison, those who wished to extricate themselves to live lives of chastity would find a new obstacle in their path.

Finally, all must face God in judgment. Judges, lawyers, and politicians who participate in the campaign to legalize homosexual "marriage" must answer for it. Catholics in the public forum, who ostensibly call Christ Lord and His Church mother and teacher, but scorn divine precepts, sin grievously. They speak from the valley of spiritual death. Should they not heed the words of the prophet Ezekiel: "But as for those whose hearts are devoted to detestable abominations, I will bring down their conduct upon their heads." Nor is this said through lack of love or concern for all. As St. Paul said: "Have I then become your enemy by preaching the truth?"

*"The narrow, closed-minded views of the National Organization for Marriage provide no rational substance to oppose gay marriage. It is my opinion that they meet the definition of bigotry."*

# The National Organization for Marriage Encourages Catholic Anti-Gay Bigotry

*Walter Barton*

*Walter Barton is a U.S. Navy veteran, a former psychotherapist, and a writer. In the following viewpoint, he argues that the National Organization for Marriage (NOM) appeals to the anti-gay bigotry of some Catholics in an attempt to prevent gay marriage. In the past, NOM has linked gay marriage to polygamy and suggested that the passage of gay marriage legislation will cause Catholic organizations to lose their tax-exempt status. Barton argues that such fear-based tactics are irrational and founded in prejudice.*

As you read, consider the following questions:

1. According to Barton, what is marriage besides a procreation activity?

2. According to Barton, why does NOM believe that same-sex marriage will lead to polygamy?

3. According to Barton, will gay marriage legislation force the Catholic Church to recognize same-sex unions?

By definition, a bigot is a prejudiced person who is intolerant of any opinions differing from [his or her] own. Having a set of beliefs, religiously or politically, that forms a unified system prevalent in a community or society is not in itself bigotry. However, when that set of beliefs creates an injustice, stigmatizes a part of the community or society, [or] makes a moral judgment on choices within that society, it becomes inconsistent with reason.

## Questions from NOM

The National Organization for Marriage, NOM,[1] provides guidelines for opposite-sex advocates of Catholic faith by posing five questions. Firstly, "How will my same-sex marriage hurt your marriage?" In their guidance, they believe proponents of same-sex marriage want to "dramatically and permanently alter" the definition of marriage and family. They believe that if same-sex marriage comes to fruition, they will be called bigots. "*The law* will teach your children and grandchildren that there is nothing special about mothers and fathers raising children together, and anyone who thinks otherwise is a bigot." In their own words, NOM professes an intolerance to providing same-sex couples from experiencing "a loving, faithful, permanent union" . . . [that helps] to satisfy men and

1. The National Organization for Marriage (NOM) is an organization that opposes same-sex marriage. It has worked with the Catholic Church to oppose gay marriage initiatives in various states.

women's "deep human longing for connection with each other," fostering commitment, trust, fidelity and cooperation. This is to say nothing of the over 1,000 benefits, rights and privileges a civilly recognized marriage . . . [garners] from the society.

NOM goes on to pose another question, "Is same-sex marriage like interracial marriage?" Their answer to the question tells us that the "laws against interracial marriage were about keeping two races apart, so that one race could oppress the other, and that is wrong." Yes, it is wrong for one race to oppress another. It is also wrong for one sexuality to oppress another. NOM continues with the set of beliefs that marriage is for procreation and . . . [to ensure that] "women aren't stuck with the enormous, unfair burden of parenting alone." I can agree marriage is a desired step in the creation of life, but it is not a requirement by law. But marriage is more than a procreation activity. It is that "deep human longing for connection with each other," fostering commitment, trust, fidelity and cooperation. And this has nothing to do with the question about interracial marriage.

## False Fears

"Is polygamy next?" NOM provides no answer to this question except to insinuate [that] same-sex marriage is similar or closely related to having more than one spouse at a time. I would think a more serious issue would have been about serial monogamy, someone like Newt Gingrich,[2] a Roman Catholic, or about pedophilia where about 50 percent of those arrested are married men and a large majority [of these men] are heterosexual.

Question 4 is "What will happen to our Catholic organizations?" NOM appears to drop the subtle fear tactic and goes directly to the emotion experienced in anticipation of the

2. Newt Gingrich was the Speaker of the House of Representatives from 1995–1999. He has been married three times.

## The National Organization for Marriage Is Not Broad-Based

"Gathering Storm" [an advertisement opposing gay marriage] was produced and broadcast—for a claimed $1.5 million—by an outfit called the National Organization for Marriage. This "national organization," formed in 2007, is a fund-raising and propaganda-spewing Web site fronted by the right-wing Princeton University professor Robert George and the columnist Maggie Gallagher, who was famously caught receiving taxpayers' money to promote [the George W.] Bush administration's "marriage initiatives." Until last month, half of the six board members (including George) had some past or present affiliation with Princeton's James Madison Program in American Ideals and Institutions. (One of them, the son of one of the 12 apostles in the Mormon Church hierarchy, recently stepped down.)

*Frank Rich, "The Bigots' Last Hurrah,"*
New York Times, *April 18, 2009. www.nytimes.com.*

dangers of gay marriage. "Legal scholars warn that the tax-exempt status and accreditation of Catholic organizations could be at risk." If any tax-exempt organization is making their property available to the public for profit, then the laws must apply to them as any other entity. The Catholic Church has legal scholars who can figure out a way to defend a bigoted viewpoint consistent with Church policy.

Lastly, NOM asks, "What will public school teach?" Instead of providing guidelines for advocates of opposite-sex marriage, NOM relies on that emotional element again. "Heather and her two mommies [3] will become standard kindergarten

3. *Heather Has Two Mommies* is a children's book by Lesla Newman. It tells the story of a little girl named Heather and her two lesbian mothers.

fare." Public schools should teach positive messages about marriage. The axiomatic idea of Heather and her two mommies not being positive is not a clever bumper sticker intended to express a general truth. It is pathetic.

NOM instills fear of same-sex marriage by a systematic set of questions designed to deceive the rational person into believing that there is some grand scheme to redefine marriage and family. . . . Same-sex marriage will only entitle unions outside the Church in the secular world. No one forces the Catholic Church to recognize those marriages. In fact, the Catholic Church believes that the union of a man and woman . . . has to be done within the Catholic Church. Nothing changes with all those non-Catholic marriages. NOM promotes the oppression of gay rights as being okay because polygamy will be next. And for good measure, NOM throws in a fear of losing tax-exempt status and public school curriculums.

The narrow, closed-minded views of the National Organization for Marriage provide no rational substance to oppose gay marriage. It is my opinion that they meet the definition of bigotry.

| "Homosexual temptation, just like any other illicit sexual temptation, should not be acted upon."

# The Catholic Church's Opposition to Gay Marriage Is Not Based on Prejudice

## Doug Williams

*Doug Williams is an information technology business analyst and the author of the blog Bogus Gold. In the following viewpoint, he argues that the Catholic Church opposes gay marriage because it does not recognize any ontological, or essential, difference between homosexuals and heterosexuals. For both, the only sexual outlet allowed is sex within a marriage that is open to procreation. Any other sexual act (including homosexual acts, adultery, or sex with a condom) is considered sinful. Williams concludes that the Church's sexual ethic is consistent, and it does not reveal a prejudice against homosexuals.*

As you read, consider the following questions:

1. According to Williams, what are some cases where society recognizes ontological distinctions but the Catholic Church does not?

Doug Williams, "The Catholic Church, Homosexuality, and Gay Marriage," Bogus Gold, April 5, 2005. Reproduced by permission.

2. According to Williams, what are some of the problems with the Church's enforcement of its sexual teachings among heterosexuals in recent years?

3. According to Williams, what is the difference in the Church's eyes between infertile married couples who engage in sex and homosexual couples who engage in sex?

One of the frustrating things in trying to explain the Church's position on homosexuality to non-Catholics, or even [to] Catholics who are less than fully informed about the Church's teaching on sexuality, is that we often talk right past one another. The problem isn't a willingness to understand or explain. It's that the difference is so fundamental [that] you'll never resolve it in the details. You must take a step back and look into the foundation.

## Men and Women Are Different

The Catholic Church teaches that men and women are onto-logically different from one another. This means there is some-thing essential to being a man that a woman does not have, and vice versa. What's more, these differences are considered "complementary." If you're thinking about the obvious bio-logical examples of this, you're on the right track, though for the Church that's not the entirety of the difference. This has serious implications when it comes to matters like the all-male priesthood, but that's a topic for another day.

The Church does not recognize this kind of distinction in other places where societies have drawn additional ontological distinctions of their own. Being of a different race is not an ontological difference according to the Church. Nor is being handicapped. Nor is being in the womb. Nor is being rich. Or poor. All are ontologically equal in the eyes of God, so the Church teaches, and [are] therefore worthy of full human rights and dignity. This is the basis of the Church's opposition to abortion, euthanasia, racial discrimination, and many other things as well.

But when we come to the case of homosexuality, two problems emerge. The first is that the Church does not recognize an ontological distinction between a homosexual and a heterosexual, whereas modern society, in creating the concept of "sexual orientation," insists there is such a distinction. Just like the Church once rejected any ontological distinction between black and white people—and therefore embraced America's civil rights movement—it rejects it as well in the case of homosexuals. Both are examples of men as good as any other in the eyes of God, and deserving of the same human rights and dignity.

If you can imagine a society [that] persecuted homosexuals merely for their "orientation," and there are many such societies in the world, you would find the Church squarely on the side of defending those homosexuals and protesting such persecution as a violation of their basic human rights.

So then we come to the next matter. If the Church rejects "orientation," how does it deal with the fact that some men are sexually attracted to other men, but not to women? Isn't it fundamentally discriminatory and unequal to allow heterosexuals a sexual outlet, but not homosexuals? The Church answers this very simply. Homosexual temptation, just like any other illicit sexual temptation, should not be acted upon.

Rather than compare this to less socially acceptable forms of sexual temptation, let's compare it to the temptation of a married man to have an affair with another woman. Quite a common temptation, it would seem. There may be more adulterers than homosexuals in our society these days for all I know. Same rule applies. Temptation doesn't excuse behavior.

## Homosexual Activity Is Like Adultery

Part of the problem for homosexuals accepting this is that the Church has been exceedingly lax [in] enforcing its own teachings regarding sexuality among heterosexuals in recent decades. This itself is a very large problem in the Church. But notice the Church's teaching here has never changed. Adultery is still a sin. Divorce is still a sin. Artificial contraception is still a sin. In fact, ignoring their duty to teach and enforce Church doctrine in this matter is also a sin for those priests and bishops charged with protecting the souls of their flock. But lazy teaching and enforcement on other matters of sexuality does not change what the Church teaches regarding homosexuality. Wrong doesn't become right just because no one in authority talks about it anymore.

Many homosexuals were outraged when the Vatican recently [2005] released a statement strongly restating the Church's teachings rejecting gay marriage while Canada debated legalizing such unions.

But in the face of the sexual revolution in the West, Pope Paul VI released [in 1968] something roughly equivalent aimed at heterosexuals: *Humanae Vitae*, an encyclical [that] strongly reiterated the Church's teachings on contraception, divorce, sex outside marriage, etc. So this kind of Vatican pronouncement in reaction to a growing societal practice against the Church's teachings regarding sexuality has precedent and is not targeted exclusively at homosexuals.

## Gay Marriage in Catholic Context

Now we come to the issue of gay marriage.

From the perspective of gay marriage advocates, marriage is the union of any two people who love and care for one another and want to form a family. Yet from the Church's perspective this definition violates two essential principles of marriage.

First, a same-sex couple is not ontologically different from one another, whereas an opposite sex couple is. That's not a small distinction to the Church. Remember, it is on this very basis that the Church defends universal rights. To agree that a homosexual is ontologically different from a heterosexual is for the Church to admit [that] homosexuals may be treated differently than other men and women. Just think of some common distinctions between men and women to appreciate the implications of this, even in a non-repressive society: separate bathrooms, certain professions barred, "gay-only" or "straight-only" exercise facilities and showers. We allow all these differences between men and women because men and women are fundamentally different, and therefore in certain areas that difference is expected to call for different treatment.

Take this the opposite direction—say there is no ontological difference between men and women. This would erase the complexity of adding new ontological distinctions by saying we're all the same. But in that case how can a "whites only" restroom be any different than a "men's only" restroom? Why are we outraged by the former and not the latter? A modern secularist might suggest it's purely due to cultural conditioning—certainly this is the radical feminist belief. Raise a boy like a girl and he'll act exactly the same as a girl raised that way. You can decide for yourself whether you share that belief. The Church does not agree and teaches that men and women, though equal in the eyes of God, are not the same thing.

The other aspect of ontology violated here is the notion of a marital couple being complementary—together the two become something neither can be on their own. And this leads directly into the next Catholic principle violated by gay marriage, which is perhaps more difficult to accept—procreation.

This one is difficult for the modern mind to grasp, because in much of the world, Catholics have ignored this teaching for decades. But the teaching remains unaltered.

In the Church's eyes, every act of sexual relations must [be] open to procreation. There is a subtle but important distinction between "open to" and "intending to." The idea isn't that you're trying to make a baby. It's that you're not intentionally doing anything to prevent it either. This answers those

## Acts Are Depraved Not People

OBJECTOR: I'm straight, but I have a lot of gay friends, and they tell me that Christians look down on them. . . . And the Catholic Church promotes this kind of hatred by its condemnation of homosexuality.

CATHOLIC: The Church is so big and so diverse that you can probably find a whole range of attitudes among its members. . . . But if we limit our discussion to the Church's *official* teachings about homosexuality, I think I can truthfully say that the Catholic Church does not hate gays nor condemn homosexuality.

OBJECTOR: Then how come the *Catechism of the Catholic Church* says that homosexual acts are "acts of grave depravity"? . . .

CATHOLIC: Homosexual acts *are* depraved, but that's not the same as saying that homosexuals are depraved. The Church, basing itself on human reason, says that in moral questions we must distinguish between the act and the person committing the act. Homosexuals have the same intrinsic dignity as all other human beings.

*Kenneth J. Howell,*
*"Does the Catholic Church Condemn Homosexuals,"*
*This Rock, July–August 2004. www.catholic.com.*

who question the Church's teaching on opposition to homosexual sex, but not sex engaged in by an infertile married couple. The difference is in willful versus involuntary infertility.

## Procreation

And why is procreation so important to the Church? Why can't it just accept the idea that a couple just wants to express their love for one another, but already has enough kids, thank you very much? Here is where the "Culture of Life" becomes more than just "opposition to death." The Church believes human life is always a good thing, and that God wants people to "be fruitful and multiply." It also teaches that the procreative act is the way God brings life into the world—remembering that, according to Christianity, human life is more than just the physical body. According to the Church, a married couple participates in God's creation of new life, but God himself is seen as the Creator of new life. Shutting the sexual act off to procreation is literally shutting out God.

I know many think this is an antiquated notion. After all, haven't standards of living reached all-time highs in countries where smaller family sizes achieved through contraception are the norm? Aren't we better now than in the old, repressive days?

Well, first, understand that the Church is more concerned about spiritual than material welfare. To gain the world but lose your soul is a losing proposition according to the Church.

Also understand that the current "baby bust" in the West is young. Already there are a lot of economists looking at the long-term implications of this with alarm. It's often called a "demographic time bomb." People openly wonder how the West will maintain its standard of living with populations that are shrinking rather than growing; and where the world consists of more and more old people, and fewer and fewer young people to support them. Some people even wonder whether "the West" will continue to exist at all, or fade away like so many civilizations in the history of the world. Perhaps there was some social wisdom to the Church's spiritual teaching as well.

So, in a rather large nutshell, there is the Catholic teaching on homosexuality that Pope John Paul II vigorously defended. Homosexual behavior is condemned (as are all acts of non-marital sex), but no homosexual person is ontologically inferior to any other human, and must be accorded equal rights and dignity. Gay marriage is not allowed because it defies the importance of ontological difference and the complementary nature of a married couple, as well as the procreative purpose of marital intercourse.

So there it is. I realize there are plenty [of people] out there who will continue to condemn the Church for hate and bigotry regardless. But at least the above will allow you to make a better-informed decision on whether you agree.

> *"What is the reason for staying in a church whose teaching on sexuality you definitively reject?"*

# Gay Catholics Should Leave the Church

*Rod Dreher*

*Rod Dreher is a conservative writer and editor for the* Dallas Morning News, *and a blogger at Beliefnet.com. In the following viewpoint, he argues that it is illogical for gay Catholics to remain in the Catholic Church if they object to its teachings on the sinfulness of homosexual acts. Dreher suggests that many gay Catholics remain in the Church because their local parishes do not preach against homosexuality or because they want to force the Church to change its ways.*

As you read, consider the following questions:

1. According to Dreher, when was the only time he heard homosexuality addressed from the pulpit?

2. According to Dreher, on what issues are most American Catholic parishes functionally AWOL?

Rod Dreher, "Why Don't Gay Catholics Leave?" Crunchy Con, November 12, 2009. Reproduced by permission of Beliefnet.com. www.beliefnet.com.

3. According to Dreher, why will orthodox religious institutions be threatened when gays have full constitutional protection?

So, why don't gay Catholics leave the Catholic Church? It could be that they are part of a parish that, in violation of Catholic teaching, affirms that their homosexuality is a moral good—in other words, they don't feel at the local level any significant pressure from Catholicism's prohibitions against homosexual behavior. (This is, I think, why so many conservative Episcopalians remain Episcopalian). It's fairly easy to live as a Catholic without having one's homosexuality (or sex life at all) come up in parish life. In all my time as a Catholic,[1] the only time I ever heard homosexuality addressed from the pulpit was two or three times at my Fort Lauderdale parish, in which the priest attacked "homophobia."

## Priests Do Not Preach Against Homosexuality

I could be wrong, but I very much doubt Andrew Sullivan[2] ever has to hear a word spoken against homosexuality at his parish in Washington, D.C. If he did, it's not hard to find parishes that don't hassle him about it, and to live one's life as an openly gay Catholic without having any kind of in-your-face conflict. In most ways dealing with the Church's hard teachings (hard for our culture to take, I mean), most American Catholic parishes are functionally AWOL. It's Moralistic Therapeutic Deism all the way down. And not just in Catholic churches, I hasten to say! The idea that poor, put-upon gay Catholics are having to sit there every week and hear priests denounce their affections from the pulpit is simply nonsense, as is the hoary pop-culture cliché that priests are obsessed with sex and harp on it in sermons. For better or for worse, that just doesn't happen.

1. Dreher was a Catholic from 1993–2002, when he converted to the Orthodox Church
2. Andrew Sullivan is a political blogger and a gay Catholic..

But the Church's principled stance against homosexuality bothers him a great deal—and it *should* bother him, given what he believes is true about homosexuality. In a case like the gay marriage referendum in Maine, in which the state's Catholic bishops lobbied against same-sex marriage, it makes perfect sense for gay Catholics who believe the Church is deeply wrong about homosexuality to be offended, inasmuch as the Catholic bishops, in fighting for what the Catholic Church teaches is true, contributed to a public policy outcome detrimental to the same-sex marriage cause. For gay Catholics, that's not nothing.

## Staying Seems Illogical

So, why do they stay in a church that condemns homosexuality *[Clarification: that condemns homosexual acts, but not homosexual persons, a distinction many gays insist is one without a difference—RD]*, and that's not going to change on the subject, when many (at least in big cities) have plenty of other options for worshiping as Christians in churches that fully affirm their sexuality? What is the reason for staying in a church whose teaching on sexuality you definitively reject (as distinct from wrestling with in good faith), and in so doing implicitly reject the Church's binding authority in matters of faith and morals? I'm not asking as a rhetorical question; I'd really like to hear what you readers—gay and straight, Catholic and non-Catholic—think. One non-Catholic reader wrote to me this morning about his own wrestling with ordination in his Protestant denomination, and how his experience arguing with church folks who doubted his motives for seeking ordination under his particular set of conditions taught him something about why gay Catholics stay:

> Over the years, I have come to realize there was probably no small measure of passive-aggressiveness in my stubbornness. I still believe the call to ministry was and is there, but I still can see some measure of seeking affirmation, even if it

meant causing a stir along the way. What I have come to realize about gay ordination as a result, even though I am not a supporter, is that what those pursuing it desire above all else is to force the Church, not only to acknowledge them, but also to *affirm* them. Thus, they act in this passive-aggressive manner and then proceed on to outright aggressiveness. They can't move on because to do so is to admit defeat in their quest for affirmation. Yes, they certainly could gain that elsewhere, but that's not what they want. They want everyone's hearts and minds, not just the like-minded. And to gain that, there is no measure of resistance they will not endure.

This, by the way, is why I have no faith at all that the Orthodox churches, synagogues, and religious institutions will be left alone once gay rights advocates have the fullest constitutional protection. Tolerance will quickly be insufficient; affirmation will be the minimal standard—or else.

> "I am not a gay Catholic at Mass. I am a Catholic. The issue of eros is trivial in the face of consecration, prayer and meditation."

# Gay Catholics Can Remain in the Church

*Andrew Sullivan*

*Andrew Sullivan is a writer and editor who blogs for the Daily Dish. In the following viewpoint, he argues that the question of gayness and sexuality is not central to the Catholic faith. As a gay Catholic, he says he stays in the Church both to work toward change and because he believes in the central tenets, promises, and experiences of the religion.*

As you read, consider the following questions:

1. According to Sullivan, in what parts of the Catholic faith does he believe?

2. As explained by Sullivan, in what parts of Catholicism does he not believe?

3. According to Sullivan, what is his main expression of alienation from the Church?

[R od] Dreher[1] is confused:

> I genuinely don't understand [Andrew Sullivan's] position. He doesn't believe the Catholic Church teaches truth, except insofar as it coincides with what he believes. Staying inside the Catholic Church makes him truly miserable. So why stay? If he wants liturgy, smells, bells, and a complete blessing on the way he chooses to live his life, there's the Episcopal Church. I actually did believe in Catholicism, but for my own reasons was so tormented by staying that I lost my faith . . . and so I left. I left in tears and heartbreak, but I left. Truly, it's a mystery to me why any free man would stay in a church in which he did not believe, and that made him so unhappy.

## Belief in Core Values

So Rod left the Church *even though he did believe*. Make what you will of that. Perhaps Rod's social or aesthetic comfort trumped his actual beliefs. We all have to follow our own path, and, unlike Rod, I am not going to peer into another's soul and make that decision for him. It is between him and his conscience.

But I want to rebut Rod's assertion that I do not "believe the Catholic Church teaches truth, except insofar as it coincides with what he believes." This is a slur, the kind of slur used by people more interested in smearing another than listening to him.

I can recite the Creed[2] with as clear a conscience as any of my fellow Catholics. I *do* believe that the Catholic Church teaches truth in the single unifying credo I can recite at every mass. I *do* believe in the message of the Gospels as deeply as I believe in anything. I *do* believe in the Catholic communion

1. Rod Dreher is a conservative writer and blogger.
2. The Nicene Creed is the profession of faith made during a service.

as the core guardian of those Gospels and of the sacraments that keep Jesus in our tangible, physical midst. And I do believe in the task of spreading God's love as the core mission of a Catholic today.

What I do not believe in are the Church's contemporary social and reactionary political positions, and its cultural hostility to women and gays, and its profound ethical corruption and sexual hypocrisy, all of which have led to astonishing scandal and evil. I do not believe that this evil should be tolerated or enabled by those who love it. And I do not believe that tackling this evil is best accomplished by leaving, as Rod, for reasons that I deeply respect, has.

In this, I try imperfectly and unworthily to follow in the wake of countless Catholics across the centuries and millennia who refused to bow down to these crass calls for total obedience from a corrupt and blinkered hierarchy when their conscience tells them it is wrong. And the idea that the Catholic Church does not accept this role for the laity is belied by the Second Council—the Council [Pope] Benedict is doing his utmost to downgrade.[3]

Sometimes, the gate is very straight—pun deeply intended. And some of us decide we would rather be constricted and conflicted in this narrow passage than avoid this spiritual challenge altogether. Because we still believe. And because this church is also *ours*.

## A Catholic, Not a Gay Catholic

Dreher follows up on his former post and wants to know why gay Catholics remain in the Church:

> I could be wrong, but I very much doubt Andrew Sullivan ever has to hear a word spoken against homosexuality at his parish in Washington, D.C. If he did, it's not hard to find parishes that don't hassle him about it, and to live one's life

---

3. The Second Ecumenical Council of the Vatican, or Vatican II, ran from 1962–1965 and liberalized or modernized a number of Church doctrines and practices.

## Homosexuals Should Be Grateful to the Church

As a Catholic and a homosexually oriented man, I am deeply grateful to the Catholic Church for her position on homosexuality and homosexual acts. Catholicism, almost alone among Christendom's churches, refuses to patronize homosexuals with a watered-down gospel or brutalize them with a message of irredeemable hostility. The Catholic Church loves me and all the men and women like me. . . . She confidently calls us to sainthood and to the narrow road that will bring us there.

*David C. Morrison,*
*"Real Love for Homosexuals,"*
*Catholic.net. www.catholic.net.*

as an openly gay Catholic without having any kind of in-your-face conflict. In most ways dealing with the Church's hard teachings (hard for our culture to take, I mean), most American Catholic parishes are functionally AWOL. It's Moralistic Therapeutic Deism all the way down.

Rod is right that most priests do not want to use the Mass [as] a means to directly hurt or abuse or berate gay parishioners. And he's right that rhetorical fulminations against gay people are very rare in my experience in the Catholic Church. But he's wrong that many of us who stay try to make an issue of it in the services we attend or even harangue fellow Catholics. I sure don't. I wore an ACT UP t-shirt to Communion once,[4] but that was the limit of my daring. I am not a gay Catholic at Mass. I am a Catholic. The issue of eros is trivial in the face of consecration, prayer and meditation.

4. ACT UP is a gay activist organization.

I write about it because I feel a need to bear witness as a gay Christian in a painful time, but mainly because I want to argue for a civil change in civil society. But it is in no way central to my faith. It is peripheral to the Gospels, is unmentioned in the Mass, and I try to focus on the liturgy and prayer and to take in as much of the sermon as is safe for my intellectual composure.

And this is not strange or, I suspect, rare for gay and nongay Catholics alike.

We all have aspects of ourselves that the Church considers inadequate or wrong. They come as a package. In my own accounting of my sins, sex does not feature much at all. Sometimes I seek a space in St. Francis's chapel, a saint I have long loved. And I try to listen to God, and pray the Lord's Prayer and meditate for a while to center myself before or after Mass. I go much less frequently than I used to, which is the main expression of my alienation, I suppose. In the summers, I barely go at all. For me the dunes are the sacraments and the water and air the incense, and the reeds the vestments, and the tides a remembrance of the change that persists. I grew up in a rural woodland and always associated it with religion and the presence of God.

So my faith life is less formal than before, less regimented, as I try to find ways of bring[ing] it more fully alive. I write these things in case people might think that the life of a gay Catholic is somehow tortured and deeply conflicted. It is conflicted, but from those conflicts can come a deeper appreciation of the truth we seek and the charity we try (and fail) to live up to.

But it [is] also true that absence from the sacrament of Communion is for me an unbearable thing after too long. Perhaps this answers something unanswerable and helps explain how many of us actually do try to live faith rather than merely assert it.

> "The presence of gay men didn't create
> the problem. The presence of homopho-
> bia created the problem."

# Homophobia and Repression Led to the Church Sex Abuse Scandal

*David France*

*David France is a contributing editor for* New York *magazine and the author of* Our Fathers: The Secret Life of the Catholic Church in an Age of Scandal. *The* Advocate *is a newspaper focused on gay issues. In the following viewpoint taken from an interview, France contends that much of the scandal around sexual abuse by priests involved gay men. However, France notes that much of this abuse was not pedophilia, in that the victims were above the age of consent. In addition, he argues that the cause of the abuse was not homosexuality itself, but rather a Catholic culture that repressed sexuality, leading gay men to lie about their sexuality to everyone—even themselves.*

As you read, consider the following questions:

1. According to France, when did the Vatican begin imposing tighter restrictions on homosexual identity?

2. According to France, why was Paul Shanley a hero?

3. According to France, was Shanley a founding member of NAMBLA?

It's easy to dismiss the child abuse scandal in the Roman Catholic Church as having little to do with gay people, because pedophiles and mature gay men are not the same thing. Right?

David France, the openly gay author of the just-published *Our Fathers: The Secret Life of the Catholic Church in an Age of Scandal*, says it's not that easy. In his exhaustively reported and intensely emotional narrative, France reveals that many of the accused priests—numbering 4,392 since 1950, according to an independent report released in February [2004]—clearly are gay men.

True, he notes, a shocking number of the abusers are villains without a clear sexual orientation, like the giggling pedophile Father John Geoghan. But many are fallen heroes, like Father [George] "Spags" Spagnolia, a social activist who briefly left the priesthood to run a guesthouse on Cape Cod, Mass., with his male partner, or Father John Shanley, a groundbreaking gay activist priest who France suggests may not be as black a villain as he's been painted.

The *Advocate* spoke to France just days before Showtime announced that it would make a cable-TV movie based on *Our Fathers....*

## Pedophilia or Homosexuality

*After the* Advocate *ran a news brief on our Web site about the murder of convicted pedophile priest John Geoghan—who was killed in prison by a serial murderer of gay men—a reader wrote to caution us against buying into the negative stereotype that links pedophilia to gay men. How would you have responded to that?*

I would respond by overstating the thesis that this is all about sexuality—every aspect of the crisis has been about homosexuality. John Geoghan was killed [because his killer believed] he was gay. He was a pedophile, and pedophilia and homosexuality are not at all related—we know statistically that gay men are less likely to be pedophiles than straight men—but the sex crisis in the Church hasn't been about pedophilia. Some 85 percent to 90 percent of all the cases of abusive priests had to do with teenagers, mostly boys.

Look, I think my knee-jerk reaction to the crisis has been the same [as your reader's]: This has nothing to do with homosexuals. But we now know from talking to these priests [who molested teenagers]: They're gay. They are gay, and the right wing knows this, and if we don't own up to those of them who are gay who did this, then nobody's going to buy our argument that the pedophiles [are not gay]. And if they were gay men, we should ask ourselves why that was happening. What caused it?

*What do you think caused it?*

What I argue is that these guys represent homosexuality in pure and total repression. This is what successful repression looks like: men so alienated from their own sense of self that their sexual expressions come out in explosive ways.

Most priests I talked to who had abused kids described the abuse as though it came upon them with the same kind of sudden surprise that it came upon their victim. This one priest, Father Neil Conway, described waking up—that's the way he described it—waking up in the middle of the sexual fondling of these kids. He really believed that he was the victim somehow—even though you have to honestly see that he created the circumstances [that led to the abuse], that he courted these kids, that he flirted with them, that he really behaved as a predator. But he couldn't see it; he was so fractured in his psyche. That's repression in its purest form.

Homosexuality has been—at least since the late '60s—a target of grave concern by Rome. The Vatican began [imposing] newer and tighter restrictions on homosexual behavior and homosexual identity in the late '60s for the first time in 400 years. As modern sexual ethics and morality began defining themselves in the '60s, the Church moved in the other direction—and in moving in the other direction it was really tearing at the psyche of its priests.

This one priest whose story I tell, Father George "Spags" Spagnolia—

*Oh, he's the most interesting priest in the book.*

He's so instructive to us on what human sexuality is all about. He joined the priesthood innocent of sexual issues. He was very young; he had never in his life masturbated. His church told him not to, and so he didn't. The Saturday after his ordination—[priests are] 26 to 28 years old at this point—he heard confession for the first time. Father Spagnolia told me he had never heard such sexual pornography as he heard that day: things he had never thought of before, ideas that had never entered his mind. He was stunned and horrified to think that this was the way the rest of the human race was comforting itself.

*But Spags went on to become a remarkable social activist—to the point that the Church drove him out of the priesthood for being too radical. And at that point, when he's no longer a priest, that's when he figures out he's gay.*

He fell in love. That struggle, that experimentation was really fascinating. But when he goes back to the priesthood he gets rid of all that other stuff. He gets rid of the *memory* of the relationship.

*To the point that he goes on the record at a press conference saying that he's always been celibate—which his ex-lover angrily denied.*

There was no need for him to do that; he just offered it up. It was the truth as he then understood it. Repression, phase 2.

## Paul Shanley, Gay Activist

*Representing the very opposite of repression is Paul Shanley, who had a long history in the '60s and '70s as essentially a gay activist.*

Paul Shanley was a hero: the first Roman Catholic priest to say anything positive about gay people—not just once or twice; he made it his career. He was traveling across the country in the early '70s, organizing conferences, speaking at the founding conference for Dignity [the organization of gay Catholics]. He was the spirit of gay rebellion: a dashingly handsome priest with a sharp tongue and no patience whatsoever with anyone who would not accept his kind of completely liberationist view of homosexuality.

For many years, during the '70s, he also ran a kind of counseling service. He took out ads in gay papers in Boston. And kids would come to him and talk about their struggles with homosexuality. His ads would say, "Gay? Bi? Confused? Call Father Paul." And these kids would come and they'd say, "I think I might be gay, and it's just destroying me because of what my church says." He'd go on and on about how they should forget the Church [on that issue]. And invariably he would make a proposal: "Well, let's just try it and see if you like it." He saw himself as some sort of a self-styled sexual liberationist.

*He appointed himself the Masters and Johnson[2] of the Catholic Church—an early sex surrogate.*

So he would have sex with these men—a kind of perfunctory sort of sex, which a lot of them are still angry about. I'm not arguing that what he was doing was any way right or

2. William Masters and Virginia E. Johnson were pioneering sex researchers.

good, but it wasn't pedophilia, and the boys he was having sex with were the age of consent and older. Now, were they consenting? Big question—we don't know. They argue in many of the suits that they weren't consenting at all. But I also include stories in the book of men who went to him for counseling and sex and were thankful for both in the end.

Then came these pedophilia charges. Three young men, now in their mid 20s, were all in the same education classes [when they were age 6 to 10]. Each of them has come to their memories of this abuse through very similar roots. They all say that they hadn't recalled the abuse [but] the details develop and clarify over time—it's a classic recovered memory. I think that in this case there's a lot to be suspicious of.

*And all three of these boys—the only three to accuse Shanley of pedophilia—are from the same very specific religious education class.*

[The accusation is that] the priest came to the class every week and took them out in threes, scattered them around the school yard and the church, played strip poker with one here while the other one's in the bathroom, went and raped—anally raped—the one in the bathroom, [then raped] the one he had stashed behind the altar, then gathered these kids up after these violent sexual violations and returned them to class—on a weekly basis. These are hour-long classes. The logistics seem illogical.

*And none of the mothers who taught the class and supervised the children remember any of this.*

None of the women who taught those classes recall it. And wouldn't the children be crying? Wouldn't the children come back in some traumatized state?

## Shanley and Alleged Child Abuse

*How long did this allegedly continue?*

## Rev. Paul Shanley's Sexual Abuse Case

Sexual abuse of minors is a real and grim problem in America. What sets the Paul Shanley case apart, however, is that it relies on uncorroborated recovered memories. To judge from press accounts, the prosecution presented no eyewitnesses, no physical evidence, no stories of contemporaneous health or emotional problems, and no recollections of unusual activity or behavior at the time. Shanley's accusers said he had removed them from catechism class regularly, sometimes weekly, in order to abuse them, but the boys' teacher said she never sent anyone to visit Shanley and that he never took anyone from class. How could such depravity go unnoticed?

*Jonathan Ranch, "Is Paul Shanley Guilty?"*
*Reason, March 14, 2005. http://reason.com.*

It began at [age] 6 and ended at 10. So four years of regular, often weekly sexual assault, often with groups. So they're going to have a lot to prove in that criminal case.

*But the troubling part, the Achilles' heel in the Paul Shanley story, is always the North American Man/Boy Love Association.*[3]

That he was [supposedly] at a meeting that somehow led to the formation of NAMBLA. That's always the glue that holds together the Paul Shanley who was the exploitative therapist with the Paul Shanley who's the accused pedophile. And it isn't true, and I spell this out in the book: NAMBLA was formed by a caucus of people meeting *after* a larger meeting that took place in Boston [which Shanley attended]. The

---

3. The North American Man/Boy Love Association (NAMBLA) argues for the liberalization of laws outlawing sexual relationships between adult men and minor males. The group has faced widespread public criticism and legal challenges.

larger meeting was about a specific legal problem in Boston that involved underage prostitutes, and there was a [smaller group] within this group that called for a caucus meeting after the conference was over. And it was [that] group of people, including Daniel Tsang, who were the founders of NAMBLA. Shanley didn't attend that side meeting.

He was quoted in a gay periodical at the time as being aggressively in defense of sexual expressions of young people. Always a dangerous line to take—it's dangerous now; it was dangerous then—to suggest that just because you're underage doesn't mean you don't have sexual agency. We don't know whether he was quoted accurately; we do know the article was written by Daniel Tsang, who was a proponent of intergenerational sex. The quotes were shocking, but he wasn't advocating the molestation of children. He was advocating the sexual agency of children. But I think once you get the NAMBLA tag attached to you, there's no getting rid of it. There's no bigger stink than that, and he hasn't been able to shake it.

*Did you talk to Shanley?*

I'm not allowed to say.

## Repression, Not Homosexuality, Caused Abuse

*The Vatican is now saying, "We wouldn't have had this problem if there hadn't been gay men in the priesthood." How is that different from what you're saying?*

The presence of gay men didn't create the problem. The presence of homophobia created the problem. The frothy, hysterical escalation against homosexual expression and homosexuality and homosexual identity by the Catholic Church, beginning in the post-Stonewall[4] era, is I think the sharpest description of homophobia we've seen in modern times. Get rid of homophobia, we wouldn't have this.

4. The Stonewall riots in 1969 were a series of violent demonstrations by gays against police persecution. They are generally seen as the starting point of the modern gay rights movement.

*In describing your book to people, I keep comparing it to Randy Shilts's* Conduct Unbecoming *or* And the Band Played On *because it has the same quality of an enormous amount of reporting at the service of very human storytelling. How many priests did you talk to?*

Scores. I talked and talked and talked. I spoke to a ton of priests and a ton of victims and a ton of lawyers in just about every part of the country, and I pared down my narrative to emotional themes. To follow [these priests] is to understand, I think, self-knowledge. Which, if that's not a gay theme—if that's not *the* gay theme I don't know what is.

> "*Access to young boys, rather than a homosexual orientation, was largely responsible for the high percentage of male abuse cases.*"

# Gay Priests Should Not Be the Focus of the Church Sex Abuse Scandal

*Daniel Burke*

*Daniel Burke is a staff writer for Religion News Service. In the following viewpoint, he reports on a study commissioned by the Catholic Church, which found that homosexual clergy were no more likely to engage in sexual abuse than were heterosexual priests. Burke also noted that some bishops were reluctant to accept the study's findings. Experts, however, noted that the findings might make it easier for some gay men to become priests.*

As you read, consider the following questions:

1. Since 1950 how much has the Catholic Church paid to settle cases of sexual abuse?

Daniel Burke, "Gay Groups Praise Report on Gay Priests and Sexual Abuse," Beliefnet, November 18, 2009. http://blog.beliefnet.com. Reprinted with permission from Beliefnet. www.beliefnet.com.

2. According to Archbishop Nienstedt, why should the Catholic Church ban gay priests if there is no link between gay priests and sexual abuse?

3. According to David Clohessy, who is really responsible for the Church's sexual abuse scandal?

Gay Catholics and victims of clergy sexual abuse are hailing preliminary results of a study commissioned by U.S. Catholic bishops that says gay priests are no more likely than straight clergy to sexually abuse minors.

Still, some bishops gathered here for the final day of their semi-annual meeting said it is premature to say whether the church leaders who had asserted such a link were wrong.

## Researchers Find No Link

Researchers from New York's John Jay College of Criminal Justice on Tuesday (Nov. 17, 2009) presented initial findings from their multi-year study of the clergy sexual abuse scandal, which has resulted in some 14,000 claims of abuse and cost the U.S. Catholic Church about $2.6 billion in settlements since 1950.

The study, which is due to be completed next year, was commissioned by the U.S. Conference of Catholic Bishops after the scandal overtook the U.S. church in 2002.

In a presentation to the bishops on Tuesday, Margaret Smith of John Jay said: "What we are suggesting is that the idea of sexual identity be separated from the problem of sexual abuse. At this point, we do not find a connection between homosexual identity and the increased likelihood of subsequent abuse from the data that we have right now."

Marianne Duddy-Burke, executive director of the gay Catholic group DignityUSA, called the report "very welcome news for gay people, gay priests, and our families and friends."

She said the John Jay report confirms other studies in concluding that sexual orientation is not connected to pedophilia

## Incidents of Reported Abuse by Priests, 1950–2002

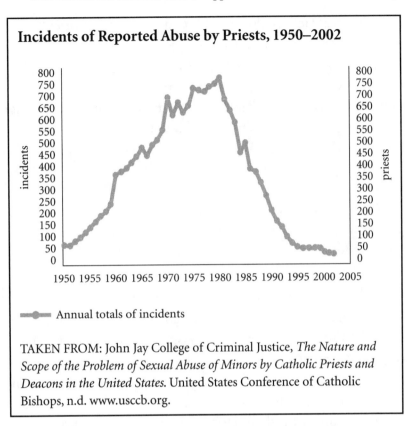

━━●━━ Annual totals of incidents

TAKEN FROM: John Jay College of Criminal Justice, *The Nature and Scope of the Problem of Sexual Abuse of Minors by Catholic Priests and Deacons in the United States.* United States Conference of Catholic Bishops, n.d. www.usccb.org.

or other sex crimes. "We hope that the hierarchy of the Catholic Church will finally accept this finding, since it has been borne out through their own study," Duddy-Burke said.

## Bishops Question Findings

Some bishops, however, said it is too early to draw conclusions about the researchers' findings.

"I wouldn't put a lot of credence in it," said Archbishop John Nienstedt of the Archdiocese of St. Paul and Minneapolis.

After the abuse crisis rocked the Church in 2002, Nienstedt helped lead a Vatican investigation of U.S. seminaries aimed at rooting out homosexuality, and served on a committee that drew up new sex-abuse prevention policies for

U.S. dioceses. He has also written that homosexual orientation is the result of childhood trauma.

Smith and her co-author, Karen Terry, stressed on Tuesday that access to young boys, rather than a homosexual orientation, was largely responsible for the high percentage of male abuse cases. "It's important to separate the sexual identity and the behavior," Terry said. "Someone can commit sexual acts that might be of a homosexual nature but not have a homosexual identity."

Still, Nienstedt said, "A priest has to be accessible to all his people, and someone with a strong same-sex attraction would not be good to have in the pastoral care of people."

Cardinal Sean O'Malley of Boston said Wednesday that the researchers' conclusions still "need to be teased out."

"I think it needs to be explained better than it was," he said. "I think that's why you saw some of the bishops challenge (the researchers)."

In 2005, the Vatican issued new guidelines barring men with "deep-seated homosexual tendencies" from the priesthood. Bishop Edward Braxton of Belleville, Ill., asked Smith and Terry on Tuesday whether homosexuality should continue to be a factor in excluding some clergy candidates.

"If that exclusion were based on the fact that that person would be more probable than any other candidate to abuse, we do not find that at this time," Smith responded.

But the view that gay men are largely responsible for the sexual abuse scandal pervades the Church hierarchy, said David Gibson, a Catholic journalist and author, and will not necessarily be overcome by the John Jay study.

"I think it will give cover to the bishops who want to continue to admit gay men into the seminary, as I think a majority of them want to do," Gibson said. "For those bishops dead set against having any homosexuals in the priesthood, it won't make a difference."

David Clohessy, national director of the Survivors Network of those Abused by Priests [SNAP], said that "the fixation on gay priests" as the cause of the sex scandal "is part of a long litany of simplistic, wrong-headed solutions and scapegoating," by the Catholic hierarchy.

"Sadly, many Catholics have already reached that conclusion though, due to the bishops' spin," Clohessy said. "The real issue continues to be the bishops' bad behavior."

# Periodical Bibliography

*The following articles have been selected to supplement the diverse views presented in this chapter.*

Brian Cavner — "Catholic Charities' Religious Freedom and Its Conflicts with Gay Marriage—A Rebuttal," *Family Fairness*, May 21, 2009. http://familyfairness.org.

Patrick J. Deneen — "Catholic Church—Same-Sex Marriage: A Threat to Social Service Contracts in D.C.?" *Washington Post*, November 12, 2009.

Mary E. Hunt — "Catholic Pride . . . and Prejudice," *Conscience*, Spring 2006. www.catholicsforchoice.org.

Michael Paulson — "Clergy Lend Voices to Marriage Debate," *Boston Globe*, April 22, 2009. www.boston.com.

Mark Pratt — "Decade in Review: Priest Sex Scandal, Gay Marriage Led Massachusetts News," *Patriot Ledger*, December 31, 2009. www.patriotledger.com.

Ronald J. Rychlak — "The Unintended Consequences of 'Same-Sex Marriage,'" InsideCatholic.com, May 2, 2008. http://insidecatholic.com.

Andrew Sullivan — "A Gay Catholic *Now*?" Daily Dish Blog, November 4, 2009. http://andrewsullivan .theatlantic.com.

Joan Vennochi — "Should Liberals Leave Catholic Church?" *Boston Globe*, March 5, 2006. www.boston.com.

Michael Sean Winters — "Wuerl Writes to Gay & Lesbian Catholics," *National Catholic Reporter*, October 8, 2009. http://ncronline.org.

Rachel Zoll — "Report: Homosexuality No Factor in Abusive Priests," ABC News, November 17, 2009. http://abcnews.go.com.

OPPOSING
VIEWPOINTS®
SERIES

CHAPTER 3

# How Should the Catholic Church Approach Reproductive and Sexual Issues?

# Chapter Preface

The Catholic Church has taken a stance against both abortion and birth control, and it often opposes sex education as well. As a result, it tends also to take a stand against population control, which usually relies on sex education, contraception, and birth control to reduce population growth, especially in poorer countries. Pope Benedict stated the Church's position, arguing that "the extermination of millions of unborn children, in the name of the fight against poverty, actually constitutes the destruction of the poorest of all human beings," as quoted by John-Henry Westen and Kathleen Gilbert in a December 13, 2008, article on LifeSiteNews.com. The pope also argued that the growth of population since World War II had been accompanied by economic advancement, and he argued that the countries with the highest birthrates are those with the most significant economic development. Thus, the pope said, "population is proving to be an asset, not a factor that contributes to poverty."

Catholics also argue that population control measures are inflicted by rich nations on poor nations, and as such are part of an "elitist, anti-life mentality," in the words of Matt C. Abbott, writing in a June 5, 2005, article on *Catholic Online*. Abbott goes on to accuse organizations like the United Nations and Planned Parenthood of being "more interested in reducing the population of those less fortunate than in working to promote authentic economic development in developing countries."

Critics of the Catholic Church have argued that its stance on population control has caused hardship in the developing world. For instance, in the Philippines, much of the population is Catholic and the Church has a strong influence on politics. Some say the Church has used this influence in part to oppose government population control initiatives. As a result, the Philippine population has one of the highest growth rates in Asia. Philippine economists and government officials have argued that this rapid growth rate "is threatening to counteract whatever economic gains the nation makes," according to a 2005 *New York Times* article by Carlos H. Conde. Elizabeth Dumaran, a government health official, is quoted in the article as stating that the Church opposes sex education and contraception, "perhaps because they don't realize what poor and large families have to go through every day."

The following viewpoints present further debate surrounding the Church's position on reproductive issues, including abortion and contraception.

| "*The Church endorses natural family planning.*"

# The Catholic Church Promotes Natural Birth Control and Sexuality Within Marriage

*Angela Townsend*

*Angela Townsend is a women's health blogger for the* Plain Dealer, *a daily newspaper in Cleveland, Ohio. In the following viewpoint, she reports on efforts by the Catholic Church to promote natural family planning (NFP). NFP is a method in which women use their body temperature in conjunction with other means to assess their own fertility and only engage in intercourse when they will not become pregnant. The Church argues that NFP is as reliable as other methods and that it allows women to avoid health issues that may arise from being on birth control pills.*

As you read, consider the following questions:

1. According to Rose Jacobs, what is the difference between natural family planning and the rhythm method?

Angela Townsend, "Catholic Church Touts Its Own Natural Plan for Effective Birth Control: Healthy Cleveland," *The Plain Dealer*, July 28, 2009. Copyright © 2008 The Plain Dealer Publishing Co. All Rights Reserved. Reproduced by permission.

2. As stated by Townsend, when did the Church formally approve standards for teaching NFP?

3. What is TeenSTAR, as explained by Townsend?

In case you didn't know, last week was Natural Family Planning Awareness Week, declared such by the U.S. Conference of Catholic Bishops.

The good folks in the office of the Diocese of Cleveland's Department for Marriage & Family Ministry wanted me to know that, especially in light of my June 23 column on the withdrawal method—"Common practice needs closer look."

They wanted to make sure that I—and everyone else— know about another kind of birth control that proponents claim is about 97 percent effective when strictly followed, without the benefit of hormonal or barrier contraception or surgical intervention.

The Church endorses natural family planning. According to literature from the diocese, "every marriage act must remain open to the transmission of life." So if a couple does not want to conceive, NFP provides guidance on when to abstain.

I checked out the diocese's Web site and was surprised to find a list of area classes, led by certified teachers, that instruct couples how to practice natural family planning correctly.

After all, there is science behind it that involves charting a woman's (basal) temperature in the morning and visually tracking changes in consistency of cervical mucus to determine her most fertile days of the month.

When those days roll around, a couple who doesn't want to get pregnant abstains from "marital acts," as Rose Jacobs, the diocese's marriage and family specialist, calls intercourse.

Of course, if the couple is ready to start or continue their family, all systems are go.

NFP is *not* the rhythm method. Jacobs cleared that up right away.

"The rhythm method itself is based on the notion that every woman has a 28-day [menstrual] cycle," she said. "NFP does not predict. It only looks at today."

The Church endorsed the rhythm method back in the 1930s. But with its less-than-ideal effectiveness rate of around 80 percent, Church leaders in the late 1960s sought assistance from Catholic scientists.

The scientists uncovered information about more "modern" forms of NFP, such as the Billings Ovulation Method, which had been developed more than a dozen years earlier. Twenty years ago, the Church formally approved national standards for teaching NFP.

"There is such a saturation of contraceptive thinking [in our culture]," Jacobs said. "We think that's a false message, to use contraception and say it's safe."

But NFP and the methods it uses are not exclusive to those who practice in the faith.

Online, many Web sites are devoted to the same or similar methods. There's a charting tool at Ovulation-calculator.com. Other sites sell digital basal thermometers and offer long explanations on the different looks of cervical mucus.

Robin Micko was 27 and newly married when she decided to explore natural family planning. It was an important part of her husband's Catholic faith. For Micko, who converted to Catholicism a few months after their marriage, not so much.

Micko jokes that she approached natural family planning "kicking and screaming."

But in reality, "I was more interested in the health benefits" of not taking hormonal contraception, she said.

Now 39, Micko and her husband have four children (two boys and two girls, ages 3, 6, 9 and 11). Their family is complete, she said.

"The nice part is, it was always about planning, always a decision that we made together," said Micko, conceding that some months were "panicky."

## The Effectiveness of Natural Family Planning

[Natural family planning] methods can help a couple avoid pregnancy if the couple receives training from a specialized instructor and if they carefully follow all of the instructions provided. . . . [The] methods can be 90% to 98% effective when they are practiced correctly. However, if a couple doesn't follow the instructions completely, these methods will be much less effective.

*FamilyDoctor.org,*
*"Natural Family Planning,"*
*April 2008. http://familydoctor.org.*

"Talk about open communication!" she said.

Some couples who need extra help with NFP turn to ob-gyn Dr. James Matheson of Vermilion.

Eight years ago, as his Catholic faith strengthened, Matheson stopped prescribing oral contraceptives and performing tubal ligations.

Today, he is one of only three northeast Ohio doctors who specialize in natural family planning.

"Over the years of practicing, I discovered a dissatisfaction [among patients], primarily with side effects [of the pill], but also with issues of how contraception affects relationships, marriages and women," Matheson said.

NFP isn't perfect—after all, the goal is to pinpoint that one day of the month when an egg can be fertilized—but it's pretty reliable when done correctly, with a success rate equal to oral contraception, he said.

And it's not just adults learning the fundamentals.

More than 10 years ago, Dr. Hanna Klaus was teaching it at St. Louis University (a Catholic college) when she decided that teenage girls—and boys—could learn it, too.

Klaus, a gynecologist, developed TeenSTAR (Sexuality Teaching in the context of Adult Responsibility), an abstinence program that goes one step further by teaching girls to chart their fertility pattern and teaching boys and girls about their bodies and responsible decision-making related to sexual behavior.

"We've always done exit questionnaires, and consistently we found that there are more [sexually active] girls who stopped [having sex after going through the program] than those who never started," said Klaus, who is now based in Bethesda, Md., as executive director of the Natural Family Planning Center and TeenSTAR program.

"That's true for boys, too," she said.

TeenSTAR classes are taught once a week for two semesters (boys and girls are in separate groups). Teachers, most of whom are volunteers, meet several times with parents and individually with students.

Although a half-dozen Catholic schools in Virginia, Dallas and Louisville, Ky., offer the program, TeenSTAR has a stronger presence in other parts of the world. In 30 countries including France, Spain, Ethiopia and Chile, 1,000 teachers in 100 different sites are teaching about 10,000 students, Klaus said.

The Mickos, who once taught NFP classes and serve on the diocese's 16-member NFP Core Committee, still field a lot of skeptical questions about their practice.

They answer thoughtful queries as well.

"We get calls all the time about it," Micko said. "It's like an underground thing that people don't like to talk about."

The Catholic Church would like to see that change.

| "Avoiding sex is something religion—
especially Catholicism—excels at."

# The Catholic Church Is Uncomfortable with Sexuality in Marriage

*Frances Kissling*

*Frances Kissling is a regular writer for* Salon.com, *and she was president of Catholics for a Free Choice from 1982 to 2007. In the following viewpoint, she argues that the Catholic Church has long avoided and feared sex. She states that this avoidance, expressed through opposition to contraception and other policies, has caused great and unnecessary suffering. She concludes by noting that most Catholics rightly follow their conscience and not the Church on such matters.*

As you read, consider the following questions:

1. According to Kissling, what should the writers of the Catholic prayer said before sex have studied in order to write something beautiful and evocative?

2. As explained by Kissling, why did early Christians feel that sex was suspect?

Frances Kissling, "New Catholic Sex Prayer—But Where's the Sex," *Salon.com*, September 22, 2009. This article first appeared on *Salon.com*, at http://www.salon.com. Reprinted with permission of the author.

3. Who is Kate Michelman and how did the Catholic Church's policy on sexuality affect her, according to Kissling?

A British publishing house has created a stir with a new book. No, not the latest teen vampire saga or best seller of intellectual derring-do; this hot commodity is the *Prayer Book for Spouses*. The 64-page booklet from the Catholic Truth Society (CTS) contains prayers about pregnancy, about caring for children and elderly parents. The prayer getting all the attention, however, is about sex. It is the prayer married couples are advised to say "before making love."

## Prayer Before Sex

It's hard not to detect a note of skepticism and confusion in media reports, as though the prayer is something akin to Scientologists using e-meters to uncover childhood secrets.[1] "The Roman Catholic Church encourages couples to pray before sex to remind themselves that intercourse is a selfless act not driven by hedonism," reads a caption in London's *Daily Mail*, which illustrates the story with a cutesy photo of a couple kneeling by a white bed. Those crazy Catholics—what will they think of next?

As for the prayer itself—well, it's gibberish. Perhaps it's unfair to subject prayers to literary criticism, but this one is a dour series of poorly strung-together clichés about married couples being mired in "half-truths and little deceits," as CTS director Fergal Martin said on the organization's Web site, adding this gloomy forecast for marriage: "For many the struggle for sincerity and truth in loving will be constant."

But more important, whoever wrote this prayer (the authors are unnamed) squeezed all the juice out of sexual pleasure. Had they bothered to study the greatest of all prayers and songs of love—the Old Testament Song of Solomon, in

1. Scientology is a religion founded by L. Ron Hubbard in 1952.

which the lover and the beloved sing to each other in 117 lines of exquisite intimacy and truth-telling—they might have written something beautiful and evocative. It could have started by drawing on the third verse: "*By night on my bed I sought him whom my soul loves.*" It could have ended as the Song of Solomon ends: "*Make haste my beloved and be thou like to a roe or to a young hart upon the mountain of spices.*" It could have invoked fine wine, the nectar of the pomegranate, the "waters that cannot quench love," the "floods that cannot drown it."

Instead the couple in the prayer whines and pleads and pretty much avoids sex altogether: "*Father, send your Holy Spirit into our hearts. Place within us love that truly gives, tenderness that truly unites, self-offering that tells the truth and does not deceive, forgiveness that truly receives, loving physical union that welcomes. Open our hearts to you, to each other and the goodness of your will. Cover our poverty in the richness of your mercy and forgiveness. Clothe us in our true dignity and take to yourself our shared aspirations for your glory, forever and ever. Mary, our Mother, intercede for us. Amen.*"

## Avoiding Sex

Avoiding sex is something religion—especially Catholicism—excels at. From the earliest days of Christianity, sex was suspect. The early Christians were sure the second coming of Jesus would happen in their lifetime and believed it was their obligation to prepare by spending as much time as possible praying and thinking about God. They understood that sex—and especially its pleasure—distracted them from that purpose. The only possible redeeming feature of sex was procreation. Just the idea of a prayer for making love would have been anathema to them: Christians were advised to avoid sex, and married couples living "as brother and sister" were the ideal. After all, Church leaders postulated that, if Adam and Eve had not sinned and had been able to remain in paradise,

## Catholics Ignore Church Teachings on Sex

In a book published in 1995, Father Andrew Greeley says surveys reveal that Catholics have sex more often, are more playful in their sex lives, and enjoy sex more than non-Catholics.

If those surveys are correct, they expose widespread hypocrisy among Catholics and a failure of the Church's "moral" teachings to influence most of them.

Despite Greeley's descriptions of sex-positive behavior, Catholic sexual doctrines are still extremely repressive. The Church denounces contraceptives, premarital sex, homosexuality, masturbation, abortion, artificial insemination, and voluntary sterilization.

*Joseph C. Sommer,*
*"Catholic Sex," HumanismByJoe.com.*
*www.humanismbyjoe.com.*

sex would be devoid of all those messy emotions—pleasure, pain, jealousy, anxiety, need. And this fear of sexual pleasure did not disappear with time. As late as the 18th century, sex was a sin outside procreation. The more pleasure you had, the more sinful it was.

Modern Catholics are embarrassed by this history. They claim everything has changed and, in some ways, it has. But even today, the Catholic Church does not accept sexuality separated from procreation. This despite the fact that most Catholic couples have sex for the purpose of having children only a few times during their married life and thousands of times as an expression of love and in pursuit of pleasure. And why not? It is incomprehensible to believe that God wishes couples to have more children than they can afford or thinks it is "good" for them to abstain from sex when they are not prepared to have children. This hostility to sexual pleasure has caused much suffering. When modern contraception became available 50 years ago, in the form of the pill, the Church forbade its use and, for a time, Catholic couples listened—often to their detriment. Kate Michelman, the former director of NARAL [Pro-Choice America, a pro-choice organization] was a young, faithful Catholic wife who used the rhythm method. She had three daughters in three years and a fourth child on the way when her husband left her. She had an abortion, a painful choice about which she has eloquently written. Today, 90 percent of Catholics in the U.S. use contraception and few of them see any need to beg for forgiveness. The principles and values that govern their sex lives are so far removed from the "prayer for spouses" that the prayer is more like a fairy tale.

## Love Does Not Require Forgiveness

Catholic couples—married, unmarried, gay and straight—feel no need for "forgiveness" for the wrongs the prayer alludes to. They do not believe their lives are impoverished. They do not feel the need to be "clothed" in dignity. Truth is found in nakedness; love itself is enriching and requires no pardon.

If anyone needs to pray for forgiveness it is popes and bishops for the pain they caused to children by scaring them into believing they'd go to hell if they masturbated, for the divorced and remarried Catholics who have been denied the sacraments, for couples who followed the teaching against contraception and had more kids than they could care for, for gay Catholics who have been denied the right to marry, and for infertile couples who are told they can't use modern fertility treatments.

The rest of us might pray that, as time marches on, more and more Catholics stop following what bishops and "spousal prayers" say on these matters—and continue to follow their common sense and their conscience.

> *"Once we cross the fundamental moral line that prevents us from treating any fellow human being as a mere object of research, there is no stopping point."*

# The Catholic Church Must Oppose Embryonic Stem Cell Research

*Nancy Frazier O'Brien*

*Nancy Frazier O'Brien is a reporter for Catholic News Service. In the following viewpoint, she reports on the U.S. bishops' condemnation of embryonic stem cell research. According to the bishops, harvesting stem cells from human embryos undermines respect for human life and suggests that the weak may be killed in the interest of the strong. The bishops also argued that using adult stem cells, the harvesting of which does not involve the loss of life, is a more ethical and more useful path for scientific research.*

As you read, consider the following questions:

1. What three educational resources did the Catholic bishops' conference plan to make available on the medical advances being made with adult stem cells?

Nancy Frazier O'Brien, "Embryonic Stem-Cell Research Immoral, Unnecessary, Bishops Say," Catholic News Service, June 16, 2008. Reproduced by permission.

2. What three arguments made in favor of embryonic stem cell research did the bishops seek to refute, according to O'Brien?

3. What "grotesque practice" was banned by the Fetus Farming Prohibition Act of 2006, according to O'Brien?

Declaring that stem cell research[1] does not present a conflict between science and religion, the U.S. bishops overwhelmingly approved a statement June 13 [2008] calling the use of human embryos[2] in such research "gravely immoral" and unnecessary.

## Nearly Unanimous Condemnation

In the last vote of the public session of their June 12–14 spring general assembly in Orlando, the bishops voted 191–1 in favor of the document titled *On Embryonic Stem Cell Research: A Statement of the United States Conference of Catholic Bishops.*

"It now seems undeniable that once we cross the fundamental moral line that prevents us from treating any fellow human being as a mere object of research, there is no stopping point," the document said. "The only moral stance that affirms the human dignity of all of us is to reject the first step down this path."

Archbishop Joseph F. Naumann of Kansas City, Kan., introduced the document on behalf of Philadelphia Cardinal Justin Rigali, chairman of the bishops' Committee on Pro-Life Activities, who was not at the Orlando meeting.

Consideration of the stem cell document came after an intense and complicated debate at the meeting over a 700-page liturgical translation. Archbishop Naumann thanked those in-

1. Stem cells are cells found in most multi-cellular organisms that have the ability to differentiate into many different cell types. They have been used to treat cancer and other illnesses.
2. Stem cells for research have in some cases been taken from human embryos, killing the embryo.

volved in the liturgical debate for "making stem cell research seem simple," which drew laughs from the other bishops.

The seven-page policy statement was approved with little debate and few amendments.

Archbishop Naumann said it would be issued in an "attractive educational brochure" intended for the "broadest possible distribution."

Also coming out this summer, he said, are three educational resources on the medical advances being made with adult stem cells: a 16-minute DVD called *Stem Cell Research: Finding Cures We Can All Live With*; an updated parish bulletin insert on the topic; and a brochure on *Stem Cells and Hope for Patients*, which will be part of the bishops' annual Respect Life observance.

## How to Pursue Progress

Although the U.S. bishops have been active in the national debate on stem cells, individually and collectively, this marks the first time they have addressed the issue in a document "devoted exclusively" to that topic, Archbishop Naumann said.

"Even our opponents admit that ours is one of the most effective voices against destroying human embryos for stem cell research," he added.

The document is designed to set the stage for a later, more pastoral document explaining why the Catholic Church opposes some reproductive technologies.

"While human life is threatened in many ways in our society, the destruction of human embryos for stem cell research confronts us with an issue of respect for life in a stark new way," it says.

"The issue of stem cell research does not force us to choose between science and ethics, much less between science and religion," the document says. "It presents a choice as to how our society will pursue scientific and medical progress."

The policy statement seeks to refute three arguments made in favor of permitting stem cell research that involves the destruction of human embryos. It says proponents of embryonic stem cell research argue:

- "Any harm done in this case is outweighed by potential benefits.

- "What is destroyed is not a human life, or at least not a human being with fundamental human rights.

- "Dissecting human embryos for their cells should not be seen as involving a loss of embryonic life."

Responding to the first argument, the document says that "the false assumption that a good end can justify direct killing has been the source of much evil in our world."

"No commitment to a hoped-for 'greater good' can erase or diminish the wrong of directly taking innocent human lives here and now," the statement adds. "In fact, policies undermining our respect for human life can only endanger the vulnerable patients that stem cell research offers to help. The same ethic that justifies taking some lives to help the patient with Parkinson's or Alzheimer's disease today can be used to sacrifice that very patient tomorrow."

On the claims that a week-old embryo is "too small, immature or undeveloped to be considered a 'human life'" or "too lacking in mental or physical abilities to have full human worth or human rights," the document notes that the embryo "has the full complement of human genes" and is worthy of the same dignity given to all members of the human family.

"If fundamental rights such as the right to life are based on abilities or qualities that can appear or disappear, grow or diminish, and be greater or lesser in different human beings, then there are no inherent human rights, no true human equality, only privileges for the strong," the statement says.

# What Are Stem Cells?

Stem cells have the remarkable potential to develop into many different cell types in the body during early life and growth. In addition, in many tissues they serve as a sort of internal repair system, dividing essentially without limit to replenish other cells as long as the person or animal is still alive. When a stem cell divides, each new cell has the potential either to remain a stem cell or become another type of cell with a more specialized function, such as a muscle cell, a red blood cell, or a brain cell.

Stem cells are distinguished from other cell types by two important characteristics. First, they are unspecialized cells capable of renewing themselves through cell division, sometimes after long periods of inactivity. Second, under certain physiologic or experimental conditions, they can be induced to become tissue- or organ-specific cells with special functions. In some organs, such as the gut and bone marrow, stem cells regularly divide to repair and replace worn out or damaged tissues. In other organs, however, such as the pancreas and the heart, stem cells only divide under special conditions. . . .

Given their unique regenerative abilities, stem cells offer new potentials for treating diseases such as diabetes and heart disease. However much work remains to be done in the laboratory and the clinic to understand how to use these cells for cell-based therapies to treat disease, which is also referred to as regenerative or reparative medicine.

*National Institutes of Health,*
*"Stem Cell Basics: Introduction,"*
*April 28, 2009. http://stemcells.nih.gov.*

## Killing Spare Embryos Is Also Unethical

The document also dismisses the argument that there is no harm in killing so-called "spare" embryos created for in vitro fertilization attempts because they would die anyway.

"Ultimately each of us will die, but that gives no one a right to kill us," the statement says. "Our society does not permit lethal experiments on terminally ill patients or condemned prisoners on the pretext that they will soon die anyway. Likewise, the fact that an embryonic human being is at risk of being abandoned by his or her parents gives no individual or government a right to directly kill that human being first."

The document also addresses moves to permit human cloning and the "grotesque practice"—banned by the Fetus Farming Prohibition Act of 2006—to develop cloned embryos in a woman's womb in order to harvest tissues and organs from them.

It closes with a reminder that the use of adult stem cells and umbilical cord blood have been shown to offer "a better way" to produce cells that can benefit patients suffering from heart disease, corneal damage, sickle-cell anemia, multiple sclerosis and many other diseases.

"There is no moral objection to research and therapy of this kind, when it involves no harm to human beings at any stage of development and is conducted with appropriate reformed consent," it says. "Catholic foundations and medical centers have been, and will continue to be, among the leading supporters of ethically responsible advances in the medical use of adult stem cells."

"While President Obama may not be making decisions in accord with the 'safer' instruction about the soul, his policy [allowing research on certain embryonic stem cells] falls within the parameters set for science by Catholic theology."

# Embryonic Stem Cell Research Can Be Reconciled with Catholicism

### Anthony Stevens-Arroyo

*Anthony Stevens-Arroyo is Professor Emeritus of Puerto Rican and Latino Studies at Brooklyn College. In the following viewpoint, he argues that, while Catholic theology says that life begins at conception, the moment of conception of embryonic stem cells is unclear. In addition, embryonic stem cells that are abandoned by the couple that created them have no chance of becoming fetuses. Given the ambiguities, and the potential for good that can come from the use of embryonic stem cells, Stevens-Arroyo argues that the use of embryonic stem cells in certain cases does not directly contradict the Catholic moral position.*

Anthony Stevens-Arroyo, "The Soul of an Embryonic Stem Cell," *The Washington Post*, March 20, 2009. Copyright © 2009, *The Washington Post*. Reproduced by permission of the author.

As you read, consider the following questions:

1. According to Stevens-Arroyo, what kind of embryonic stem cell research did George W. Bush ban and what kind did he not regulate?

2. According to Stevens-Arroyo, why has the Catholic Church traditionally spoken out against in vitro fertilization?

3. According to Stevens-Arroyo, why is it important that potential human beings share rights with actual human beings?

When President [Barack] Obama revoked a ban on federal funding for embryonic stem cell research [in March 2009] he invited some pro-life bloggers to claim again that he is a "baby killer." The controversy is not new. When still a candidate [in 2008], Obama indicated he would reverse the prohibition that [President George W.] Bush had decreed on government-sponsored research with embryos. (Bush did nothing about privately funded, for-profit research). This is certainly a moral issue that walks the boundary line that separates church from state because no one claims the government or private enterprise has a license to kill a living person. But is an embryo a human person? When asked by Pastor Rick Warren [an American evangelical Christian minister and author] about this issue, candidate Obama indicated that decisions about when conception takes place were above his "pay grade." This is rare humility for any politician.

## Theology and Biology

Catholic theological teaching is unequivocal: The human soul is infused by God at the moment of conception. The biological issue of when exactly conception can be considered to have occurred is less clear. Cardinal [Justin] Rigali, head of the U.S. bishops' committee on such matters, has quoted some doctors who make fertilization of the embryo the moment of conception. Those embryos have souls, it would be said. Other doctors, perhaps a majority of fertility experts, state conception takes place only after that fertilized embryo is implanted in the womb and grows as a fetus.

Which medical opinion should the Church follow? Is the person in an embryo or only in a fetus? To avoid this dilemma, the Church has long spoken against in vitro fertilization.[1] But recognizing the moral issues of the world, the late Pope John Paul II appointed a Pontifical Commission of doctors to offer informed opinions on the biological issues. After admitting that there were sound arguments for both moments, they recommended that the Church take the "safer" position of a soul to the embryo, rather than the fetus. But "safer," *tutior* in Latin, means that the other position is still "safe."

Critics of the Church's position often accuse Catholicism of protesting stem cell research out of a malevolent or medieval obsession. However, it would be a fallacy to say that Catholicism is against stem cell research: only the embryonic stem cells present the moral dilemma. Catholics agree that scientific research on stem cells is valuable, but they want to use adult stem cells, not the embryos. The *tutior* position of the Church says that even if an embryo may not be a human person in a biological sense, it has the potential of becoming so. In Catholic theology, potential human beings share rights with actual human beings. That principle should be upheld by every Catholic, for otherwise the door is opened to the murder of people on life support, the impaired and the like.

## Lost Potential

However, the abandonment of embryos by couples who have decided not to use these frozen stem cells has created a new situation. If the law makes it impossible for these embryos to

---

1. In vitro fertilization is when eggs are fertilized by sperm outside the womb and are then implanted in the uterus. It is a common infertility treatment.

## Obama Funds Embryonic Stem Cell Research

The [Barack] Obama administration has begun approving new lines of human embryonic stem cells that are eligible for federally funded experiments, opening the way for millions of taxpayer dollars to be used to conduct research that was put off-limits by President George W. Bush.

Launching a dramatic expansion of government support for one of the most promising but most contentious fields of biomedical research, the National Institutes of Health on Wednesday [December 2, 2009] authorized the first 13 lines of cells under the administration's policy and was poised to approve 20 more Friday.

*Rob Stein,*
*"U.S. Set to Fund More Stem Cell Study,"*
Washington Post, *December 3, 2009.*
*www.washingtonpost.com.*

be used except by a deceased couple who no longer pay to have them preserved, have they lost the potential to grow into human beings by artificial insemination? If they are otherwise to be destroyed, then does not the good that can be done to heal disease outweigh protecting a nonexistent potential? Theologians must advise the bishops that there is a difference between metaphysical potentiality and this specific case. Metaphysical potentiality says: "Any child born in the United States can grow up to be president." But this generality evaporates in the specific case of a Down syndrome child.

These are deep, delicate and daunting issues. They are not resolved by "baby killer" accusations or by cavalier dismissal of Catholic moral concern. While President Obama may not be making decisions in accord with the "safer" instruction about the soul, his policy falls within the parameters set for science by Catholic theology. And maybe it should be that way. I'd hate to see a president invoking theology as a basis for policy: that would turn the democracy into a theocracy. A better political course would be for Catholic America to press for research into the use of non-embryonic stem cells, transforming a divisive issue into one focused on healing the sick.

"If men did not stray, if women had rights, if AIDS did not kill, perhaps the Church's strict ban on condom use would be morally defensible. But none of these conditions applies in Africa today."

# The Catholic Church's Opposition to Condoms Endangers African Women

*Marcella Alsan*

*Marcella Alsan, MD, is a physician in the Hiatt Residency in Global Health Equity and Internal Medicine at Brigham and Women's Hospital, Boston. In the following viewpoint she argues that, contrary to the Catholic Church's contentions, condom use has been shown in numerous studies to substantially reduce the risk of HIV infection. She also notes that most of those infected by HIV in Africa are married women whose husbands have been unfaithful. Thus, the Catholic Church's argument that AIDS is caused by sexual immorality does not apply to most victims, who have not been immoral themselves. Alsan concludes that in opposing condom use the Church is betraying its own commitment to life.*

As you read, consider the following questions:

1. According to Alsan, in South Africa how many people are infected with the AIDS virus and what percentage of pregnant women?

2. According to Alsan, what may have caused the upswing in cases of HIV in Uganda?

3. According to Alsan, what sort of misconceptions do young people have about AIDS?

As a young physician, I often second-guess myself. In practicing medicine such self-criticism is warranted, even obligatory, because a wrong diagnosis can lead to misguided therapy and may end in death. After working at a Catholic hospital in the small sub-Saharan country of Swaziland, however, there is one diagnosis I pronounce with uncharacteristic certitude: AIDS.

## AIDS Strikes Married Women

The typical patient is a young woman between eighteen and thirty years of age. She is wheeled into the examining room in a hospital chair or dragged in, supported by her sister, aunt, or brother. She is frequently delirious; her face is gaunt; her limbs look like desiccated twigs. Surprisingly, the young woman is already a mother many times over, yet she will not live to see her children grow up. More shocking still, she is married; her husband infected her with the deadly virus.

This is the reality: A married woman living in southern Africa is at higher risk of becoming infected with HIV than an unmarried woman. Extolling abstinence and fidelity, as the

Catholic Church does, will not protect her; in all likelihood, she is already monogamous, it is her husband who is likely to have HIV. Yet refusing a husband's sexual overtures risks ostracism, violence, and destitution for herself and her children. Given these realities, isn't opposing the use of condoms tantamount to condemning countless women to death? In the midst of the AIDS epidemic, which has already killed tens of millions and preys disproportionately on the poor, the condom acts as a contra mortem [guard against death] and its use is justified by the Catholic consistent ethic of life.

At least, this is the view of many Catholics at the front lines of the global HIV battle. Catholic organizations mercifully provide around 25 percent of the care AIDS victims receive worldwide. Many of the clergy and laity involved in treating people with AIDS, who otherwise fully ascribe to the Church's teachings on sexual ethics and the sanctity of marriage, nevertheless endorse the use of condoms. They argue that the preservation of human life is paramount. Fr. Valeriano Paitoni, working in Sao Paulo, Brazil, summarized this perspective: "AIDS is a world epidemic, a public health problem that must be confronted with scientific advances and methods that have proven effective," he says. "Rejecting condom use is to oppose the fight for life."

Bishop Kevin Dowling of South Africa has also been imploring the Vatican to view condom use as curtailing the transmission of death rather than precluding the transmission of life. In South Africa, 5.3 million people are infected with HIV and 25 percent of all pregnant women test positive for the virus. Dowling prays that the Holy Spirit will intervene to change minds in Rome. He believes Pope Benedict XVI's view on the use of condoms would change, "if his visits to poor countries were done in such a way that he could sit in a shack and see a young mother dying of AIDS with her baby." Not long ago, Belgian Cardinal Godfried Danneels stated on Dutch television that although sex with a person infected with HIV is to be avoided, "if it should take place, the person must use a condom in order not to disobey the commandment condemning murder, in addition to breaking the commandment which forbids adultery." He added: "Protecting oneself against sickness or death is an act of prevention. Morally, it cannot be judged on the same level as when a condom is used to reduce the number of births."

## The Vatican Will Not Compromise

Unfortunately, the Vatican has not budged. Condoms thwart conception; therefore, by the 1968 encyclical *Humanae Vitae* [a papal document that reaffirmed the Church's position on abortion, contraception, and similar issues], their use is proscribed. End of debate. In a 2003 Vatican document titled *Family Values Versus Safe Sex*, the use of condoms in HIV-prevention programs was forcefully rejected:

> The Catholic bishops of South Africa, Botswana, and Swaziland categorically regard the widespread and indiscriminate promotion of condoms as an immoral and misguided weapon in our battle against HIV/AIDS for the following reasons. The use of condoms goes against human dignity. Condoms change the beautiful act of love into a selfish search for pleasure—while rejecting responsibility. Condoms do not guarantee protection against HIV/AIDS. Condoms may even be one of the main reasons for the spread of HIV/AIDS.

Cardinal Alfonso López Trujillo, head of the Pontifical Council for the Family, has elaborated on the latter point: "In the case of the AIDS virus, which is around 450 times smaller than the sperm cell, the condom's latex material obviously gives much less security . . . to talk of condoms as 'safe sex' is a form of Russian roulette." Trujillo called on ministries of health to require "a warning, that the condom is not safe" on packages distributed worldwide.

Although it is true that condoms are not 100 percent effective in preventing HIV infection, they do reduce the risk of transmission significantly. Comparing condom use to a suicidal dare, as Cardinal Trujillo does, is scientifically inaccurate and socially irresponsible. A preponderance of medical research demonstrates that condoms help prevent the spread of HIV. For example, the European Study Group on Heterosexual Transmission of HIV followed 124 discordant couples (in which only one of the pair is infected with HIV) who consistently used condoms. Over a two-year period and roughly fifteen thousand sexual acts, none of the HIV-negative partners contracted the virus. Thai investigators examining the impact of condom use among the military reported that new infections dropped from 12.5 percent in 1993 to 6.7 percent in 1995. The number of new HIV infections in Thailand plummeted after the introduction of a "100 percent condom use" program. Uganda earned its reputation as a paragon of HIV prevention for its now-famous ABC program: Abstinence, Be faithful, and Consistent, Correct use of Condoms. Following the implementation of ABC, HIV infection in Uganda decreased from between 15 and 20 percent of the population in the early 1990s to 5 percent in 2003. A comparative analysis of Ugandan population-based surveys in 1989 and 1995 concluded that delaying the age of first sexual encounters, decreasing the number of casual partners, and increasing condom use all contributed to Uganda's success. More recently, though, HIV has been on the rise in Uganda. Current data estimate 7 percent of the population is infected with the AIDS virus. Some advocacy groups attribute this upswing to a national condom shortage orchestrated by the Ugandan government under pressure from the Bush administration. The Health Ministry of Uganda refutes this allegation, stating that delays in the distribution of condoms have been the result of enhanced inspection of shipments after a batch of Chinese condoms was purportedly discovered to be faulty.

## AIDS in Selected African Countries at the End of 2008

| | People with HIV-AIDS | Adult % | Women with HIV/AIDS | Children with HIV/AIDS | AIDS Deaths | Orphans due to AIDS |
|---|---|---|---|---|---|---|
| Botswana | 300,000 | 23.9 | 170,000 | 15,000 | 11,000 | 95,000 |
| Cote d' Ivoire | 480,000 | 3.9 | 250,000 | 52,000 | 38,000 | 420,000 |
| Ghana | 260,000 | 1.9 | 150,000 | 17,000 | 21,000 | 160,000 |
| Nigeria | 2,600,000 | 3.1 | 1,400,000 | 220,000 | 170,000 | 1,200,000 |
| South Africa | 5,700,000 | 18.1 | 3,200,000 | 280,000 | 350,000 | 1,400,000 |
| Uganda | 1,000,000 | 6.7 | 520,000 | 110,000 | 91,000 | 1,000,000 |
| All of Sub-Saharan Africa | 22,000,000 | 5.0 | 12,000,000 | 1,800,000 | 1,500,000 | 11,600,000 |

TAKEN FROM: Avert, "AIDS and HIV Statistics for Sub-Saharan Africa," [2009]. www.avert.org.

## Abstaining Is Not an Option

Of course, never having sex will significantly reduce the risk of contracting a sexually transmitted disease. (It will not, though, completely eliminate the risk of contracting HIV, since the virus is also transmitted via blood products, birthing, and breastfeeding.) But the Vatican must be made aware that abstaining from sex is not a choice that many women living in the developing world have. To preach fidelity and abstinence assumes that a woman can determine with whom she sleeps and when—a grave misunderstanding of the relations between the sexes in places where women are sometimes betrothed at birth or sold for cattle. How can the Vatican continue to prohibit the use of a life-saving intervention amid a pandemic of unprecedented proportions? By reflexively invoking *Humanae Vitae* whenever the condom issue arises, the Church has tragically misdiagnosed the moral problem at hand.

Benedict XVI made his first comments as pope regarding condom use at a June 2005 papal audience. His listeners included bishops from South Africa, Swaziland, Botswana, Namibia, and Lesotho. After reviewing the importance of catechesis [religious instruction] and recruiting African men to the priesthood, the pope turned his attention to AIDS: "It is of great concern that the fabric of African life, its very source of hope and stability, is threatened by divorce, abortion, prostitution, human trafficking, and a contraception mentality." He emphasized that contraception leads to a "breakdown in sexual morality." In the speech, the pope made a diagnosis: Condoms increase sexual immorality, and sexual immorality increases the spread of AIDS. The logical treatment for sexual immorality is Christian marriage, fidelity, and chastity. Cardinal Javier Lozano Barragán, president of the Vatican's [Pontifical] Council for the Pastoral Care of Health Care Workers, had reached a similar conclusion in his Message for World AIDS Day (December 1, 2003): "We have to present this [lifestyles emphasizing marriage, fidelity, and chastity] as the main way for the effective prevention of infection and spread of HIV/AIDS, since the phenomenon of AIDS is a pathology of the spirit."

Fidelity in marriage and abstinence for everyone else would be the only indicated intervention if a "pathological spirit" were the only cause of AIDS. Unfortunately, many victims of HIV are blameless. Currently, 25 million HIV-infected individuals and 12 million AIDS orphans are living in sub-Saharan Africa. The communities hardest hit by AIDS are among the world's most impoverished. Sub-Saharan Africa, which has the world's lowest per capita annual income ($450 US), and where half of all individuals live in extreme poverty (earning less than a dollar a day), is ground zero of the epidemic. Over 70 percent of all infections, 80 percent of all AIDS-related deaths, and 90 percent of all AIDS orphanings occur here. And with over six thousand new infections per day, the epidemic shows no signs of abating.

Obviously, the poor are limited in their access to education and to health services. Ignorance kills. When accurate information is not available, myths multiply. Surveys from forty countries indicate that more than 50 percent of young people aged fifteen to twenty-four have serious misconceptions about how HIV/AIDS is transmitted. Research by the Nelson Mandela Foundation has shown that 35 percent of twelve- to fourteen-year-olds thought that sex with a virgin could cure AIDS, or were unsure whether or not that statement was true. In other impoverished nations, AIDS is thought to be spread by witchcraft, mosquito bites, or through polio vaccination.

As already noted, the Church in Africa is facing a grim reality even when it comes to sex in marriage. According to UNICEF [the United Nations Children's Fund], teenage brides in some African countries are becoming infected with the AIDS virus at higher rates than sexually active unmarried girls of similar ages. That's because young brides are acquiring HIV from their husbands, who tend to be many years older and were infected before marriage. Clearly, abstinence and fidelity prevention strategies will not reliably protect these women. The result is reflected in the epidemiology of the disease: More than two-thirds of new HIV infections among people aged fifteen to twenty-five occur among women. In some areas of Africa, girls are five to six times more likely to be HIV-positive than boys of the same age.

## Poverty, Racism, Gender, and AIDS

The suffering associated with these alarming trends is difficult to comprehend. Stephen Lewis, UN special envoy for HIV/ AIDS in Africa, summarized it this way: "To this catalogue of horrors, there must be added, in the case of Africa, that the pandemic is now, conclusively and irreversibly, a ferocious assault on women and girls." What has been called the "feminization of poverty" is a particularly lethal phenomenon in conjunction with AIDS. Gender discrimination in much of the world prohibits women from owning property or earning a living wage. To survive these harsh economic realities, many women are forced into prostitution. Paul Farmer, the Harvard physician and anthropologist, has noted that the women he interviewed in Haiti "were straightforward about the nonvoluntary aspect of their sexual activity: In their opinions, poverty had forced them into unfavorable unions. Under such conditions, one wonders what to make of the notion of 'consensual sex.'"

In Africa, the legacy of colonial racism, and especially of apartheid, still plays a role in determining one's risk of contracting HIV. In South Africa, a migrant labor system separated husbands from wives and made normal family life impossible. That pattern continues in the mining industry today, where the conflation of harsh working conditions, separation from wife and family, and the invariable proximity of brothels facilitate the spread of HIV from sex worker to laborer, and thence to his wife and children.

Acknowledging the roles that poverty, racism, and gender inequality play in fueling the spread of AIDS in no way diminishes the need for personal responsibility and moral restraint. Indeed, even the correct and consistent use of condoms will require behavior change and individual accountability. But by narrowly diagnosing AIDS as a problem of morality and by discrediting a vital component of HIV prevention, the Church is advancing a remedy that is woefully inadequate. In medicine, partial therapy is at best ineffective—and at worst lethal.

If men did not stray, if women had rights, if AIDS did not kill, perhaps the Church's strict ban on condom use would be morally defensible. But none of these conditions applies in Africa today. As a consequence, the cost of the Church's inflexibility may mean not only untold human suffering, but the loss of millions of innocent lives.

> *"The idea that faithful Roman Catholics would follow rules regarding the use of condoms, but ignore the more important doctrines of marital fidelity is ludicrous, at best."*

# The Catholic Church Is Not Responsible for the Spread of AIDS in Africa

*Rich Deem*

*Rich Deem is not a Roman Catholic but a Protestant. His rebuttal of the idea that the Catholic Church's condom policy is responsible for the spread of AIDS should not be interpreted as general support of the Catholic Church. Rich Deem is a researcher/specialist in the Inflammatory Bowel Disease Center at Cedars-Sinai Medical Center and writes on God and science for the Web site Evidence for God from Science. In the following viewpoint, he argues that it is illogical to believe that faithful Catholics would obey the Church in regard to condom use, but they would not obey in regard to fidelity. He also points to sta-*

Rich Deem, "Is the Roman Catholic Church's Condom Policy Responsible for the Spread of HIV and the AIDs Crisis in Africa?" Evidence for God, May 2, 2008. Reproduced by permission. www.godandscience.org.

*tistical evidence showing that Catholic areas of Africa do not have higher incidences of AIDS than non-Catholic areas. He concludes that Catholic teachings are not responsible for AIDS in Africa.*

As you read, consider the following questions:

1. According to Deem, what is the only form of birth control that is not a sin?

2. According to Deem, why do the unfaithful commit adultery?

3. According to Deem, are rates of AIDS higher, lower, or the same in Catholic countries as in non-Catholic countries, and is this trend statistically significant?

The claim that the teachings of the Roman Catholic Church are at least partly responsible for the spread of AIDS in Africa is one of my favorite myths among atheists. It is remarkably prevalent among people who should know better, had they thought about it for more than five seconds. The assertion goes something like this. The Catholic Church teaches that faithful Catholics should not use any form of birth control, including condoms. Since faithful condom use prevents the vast majority of instances of transmission of the HIV virus, the Catholic Church is responsible for some, if not most, instances of AIDS in Africa. On the surface, it seems like a logical argument, except something is missing. . . .

## Teachings of the Catholic Church

Yes, it is true that the Roman Catholic Church teaches that any form of birth control, other than natural family planning . . . is a sin. This teaching comes from several sources, but begins in the very first chapter of the very first book of the Bible, Genesis. God's first commandment to human beings, immediately after they were created was to have sex, through

## Condoms Are Not the Solution in Africa

The unavoidable fact is that, in Africa, AIDS transmission rates have increased alongside the promotion of condoms. In Africa condoms cannot be used in the way that gay people use them in San Francisco, because the context is quite different. Condoms are not easily available, on a regular basis. They cannot readily be afforded, when not supplied. And even when they are available, the motivation is often lacking. What drives promiscuity is not hedonism, but desperation and despair.

*Austen Ivereigh,*
*"On Condom Use, the Pope May Be Right,"*
Guardian, *March 19, 2009. www.guardian.co.uk.*

the command to multiply and fill the earth. The command was clarified in the second chapter of Genesis, where it was made clear that husbands and wives were to engage in sexual relations to produce children. However, not all Christians agree that the use of birth control is a sin.

If Roman Catholics are so faithful in their obedience to the Church's teaching on birth control, one would think that they would want to obey the Church's other, more important teachings about sexuality. The Roman Catholic Church (and virtually all Christian denominations) says that sexual relations are to be reserved for husbands and wives within a monogamous marriage. In fact, this doctrine is a cornerstone teaching from the original Ten Commandments. So, according to the hypothesis, faithful Roman Catholics will not use a condom because of the Church's teachings, but will commit the greater sin of adultery. In reality, it is the unfaithful who commit adultery. The reason they don't use a condom is be-

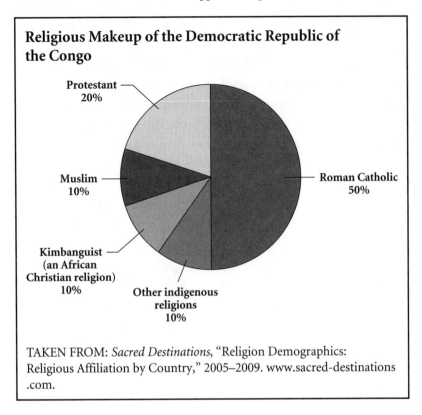

**Religious Makeup of the Democratic Republic of the Congo**

TAKEN FROM: *Sacred Destinations*, "Religion Demographics: Religious Affiliation by Country," 2005–2009. www.sacred-destinations .com.

cause they don't care about their spouses, but are simply interested in their own pleasure. Let's face it, condoms just aren't as much fun.

## Catholicism vs. HIV Infection Rate

If Roman Catholicism is responsible for the AIDS epidemic in Africa, it would be a fairly trivial matter to test the hypothesis. The percentage of Roman Catholics in various countries of Africa are quite diverse, as are the HIV infection rates. One need only plot the percent Catholics vs. the HIV infection rate.... If the hypothesis that Catholic doctrine spreads HIV and AIDS, we would expect to see *increased* infection rates in countries that contain more Roman Catholics. Instead, we find *decreased* HIV rates in Catholic-dominated countries (although the trend is not statistically significant). The idea that Roman Catholic teaching encourages the spread of HIV is not confirmed by the demographics.

The hypothesis that the Roman Catholic doctrine against the use of condoms facilitates the spread of HIV and AIDS is formally falsified through available demographics. If anything, Roman Catholicism seems to decrease the spread of HIV. The idea that faithful Roman Catholics would follow rules regarding the use of condoms, but ignore the more important doctrines of marital fidelity is ludicrous, at best. So, Roman Catholicism isn't the cause of the AIDS crisis in Africa. Get over it!

> "We who know the truth that every pro-cured abortion takes an innocent hu-man life cannot participate in any new health care plan that includes anti-life procedures under its definition of 'health care services.'"

# The Catholic Church Must Prevent Abortion Being Funded Through Health Care Reform

*Keith Fournier*

*Keith Fournier is a deacon who writes regularly for the Web site Catholics Online. In the following viewpoint, he argues that President Barack Obama and the U.S. Congress are on their way to passing a health care bill that will use taxpayer money to pay for abortion services. Fournier adds that there is no clause in the bill allowing health care providers to refuse to provide abortion services if they have moral objections. Fournier concludes that any such state-sponsored abortion services are unacceptable and immoral, and he calls on pro-life supporters to organize to pre-vent the bill from passing.*

Keith Fournier, "Massive Resistance! 'Health Care' Funds Abortion?" Catholic Online, July 18, 2009. Article provided by Catholic.org. Reproduced by permission.

As you read, consider the following questions:

1. According to Fournier, who has been responsible for the most effective effort to prevent the inclusion of abortion in the health care bill?

2. Do the Catholic bishops support reforming the nation's health care system, according to their statement?

3. What does Fournier suggest that pro-life individuals do in order to show their opposition to the proposed health care reform bill?

The President of the United States [Barack Obama] is proceeding rapidly with health care reform [as of July 2009]. It appears that it will soon become the law of the land.

## An Abortion Emergency

Concerns over the centralization of such a major new program within the increasingly bloated federal bureaucracy, questions concerning violations of the principle of subsidiarity in its implementation, and worries as to whether such an approach can provide efficiency and economy of scale are all legitimate. However, they simply are not carrying the day.

What leads me to write this [viewpoint] and sound the alarm is that an emergency looms as a result! The destruction of the lives of millions of our first neighbors, children in the first home of the womb, funded with taxpayer money, appears to be a part of this plan.

The current unavailability of health care to many is simply unjust. Most people acknowledge that the current method of delivering health care services must be reformed. This [viewpoint] deals with reality. Some version of the presidents' plan will pass. For Catholics, other Christians, (that is at least Christians who still adhere to the unbroken teaching concerning the dignity of every human person at every age and stage and have not compromised the truth), other people of faith and all people of goodwill who recognize the preeminent natural law right to life and the foundational freedom to be born, there is a resulting looming emergency. This health care bill is about much more than the economic implications and loss of local control. *This has become a matter of life and death.*

The truth must be faced, abortion, other anti-life procedures and the deadly misuse of some technologies will soon, short of a major change, be treated as "health care services" to be covered under this new plan, funded with taxpayer dollars. All of this without the so called "robust conscience clause"[1] promised by the president! If I am wrong, I truly welcome being corrected. At this point, the most effective effort to deal with this matter of life or death seems to be the twenty pro-life House Democrats who sent a letter to their colleagues on Friday [July 2009] stating they "cannot support any health care reform proposal unless it explicitly excludes abortion from the scope of any government-defined or subsidized health insurance plan."

## No Subsidies for Abortion

Democratic Representative Bart Stupak of Michigan, one of the signers, said "I told leadership repeatedly, but they just sort of ignored us. . . . They ignore at their own peril." The late great Governor Bob Casey [governor of Pennsylvania from 1987 to 1995 and pro-life Democrat who contemplated running for president] the last Democrat I supported for president, would be proud of these committed Democrats who hear the cry of all the poor. I hope that they, along with the efforts of heroes for life such as Chris Smith [House Representative from New Jersey] in the Republican Party, can prevail. However, we must be ready for the worst.

In a July 26, 2009, press release, Bill Donohue, the president of the Catholic League [for Religious and Civil Rights]

---

1. A conscience clause would allow Catholic health care providers to refuse to perform abortion-related services.

## The Proposed Stupak Amendment

Under our amendment [an amendment to the health care reform bill, proposed by representatives Bart Stupak and Joseph R. Pitts] women who receive federal subsidies will be prohibited from using them to pay for insurance policies that cover abortion. The amendment does not prevent private plans from offering abortion services and it does not prohibit women from purchasing abortion coverage with their own money.

Bart Stupak, *"What My Amendment Won't Do,"*
New York Times, *December 8, 2009. www.nytimes.com.*

summarized the situation well: "Exactly two weeks ago today, President Obama met with some Catholic journalists, telling them, 'I don't know any circumstances in which abortion is a happy circumstance or decision,'" said Donohue. "This begs the question: Why are his surrogates in the Democratic Party pushing to make the public pay for a procedure that always makes women (and children) so unhappy?" Donohue noted that amendments offered by Sen. Orrin Hatch and Sen. Mike Enzi that would have prohibited the public funding of abortion in the health care bill were struck down, "all to the applause of the Obama administration."

He continued: "Something has got to give. If abortion is bad, then it makes no sense to subsidize it," said Donohue. "After all, there is a reason why we don't subsidize air or water pollution." In addition, said Donohue, Obama appears not to be keeping his famed pledge at Notre Dame for a "sensible conscience clause" to "honor the conscience of those who disagree with abortion. . . . This begs the question: Why are his surrogates in the Democratic Party pushing to kill conscience rights? To be exact, yesterday [July 17, 2009] the Democrats killed an amendment by Sen. Tom Coburn to provide conscience-rights protections for health care workers. This is a break point for Obama and Catholics. The president either means what he says when he talks to Catholics, or he doesn't."

On May 20, 2009, all of the U.S. Catholic bishops, speaking through Bishop William F. Murphy, the chairman of their Committee on Domestic Justice and Human Development, placed a statement in the *Congressional Record* at a formal roundtable discussion on "Expanding Health Care Coverage." Along with some helpful proposals to guide honest health care reform it included this clear and unequivocal statement:

> "While we support reforming our nation's health care system, we must also be clear in strongly opposing inclusion of abortion as part of a national health care benefit. For decades, Congress . . . has decided not to compel people to pay for abortions with their tax dollars, and this policy should remain in place. We also oppose inclusion of other procedures or technologies that attack or undermine the sanctity and dignity of life. No health care reform plan should compel us or others to pay for or participate in the destruction of human life. To preserve this principle is morally right and politically wise as well. No health care legislation that compels Americans to pay for or participate in abortion will find sufficient votes to pass."

## Massive Resistance

Sadly it appears that the president and Congress have disregarded our bishops. They have also disregarded every American who supports the fundamental right to be born in this country. They appear ready to "compel us or others to pay for or participate in abortion." Every Catholic, other Christian, other person of faith and person of good who knows the truth about what is at stake must be prepared to refuse to participate in any "health care" system that funds the taking of innocent human life. We should consider ways we can band together to support one another in this resistance and provide alternatives for the medical care of people who participate in this just cause. Perhaps there will need to be a medical underground railroad for those medical practitioners who understand their oath and refuse to participate in the taking of human life.

There is an irony to my timing in writing this somber piece. I just yesterday wrote about the misguided fears that too often paralyze so many of us. However, this warning is not an effort to elicit fear, but a realistic call to preparation for action. Short of a miracle, which I truly do believe in, we will soon face a time of necessary massive resistance. We who know the truth that every procured abortion takes an innocent human life cannot participate in any new health care plan that includes anti-life procedures under its definition of "health care services."

> "Why . . . has Catholic ethical concern
> been so allowed to narrow as to have
> become shriveled?"

# The Catholic Church Should Not Make Abortion Central to Health Care Reform

## James Carroll

*James Carroll is a columnist for the* Boston Globe *and the author of* Practicing Catholic. *In the following viewpoint, he argues that, in its singular focus on abortion, the Catholic Church has abandoned its traditional concern for the common good. He argues that Catholic bishops should be engaged with the social evils caused by unemployment and anti-immigration legislation. He concludes that the Church has been taken over by fringe elements. As evidence, he points to American bishops' willingness to abandon the goal of broader health care on the grounds that the bill includes funding provisions for abortion.*

As you read, consider the following questions:

1. What topics are discussed in Pope Benedict's encyclical *Charity in Truth*, as explained by Carroll?

James Carroll, "The Church's Abortion Mistake," *The Daily Beast*, November 10, 2009. Reproduced by permission.

2. According to Carroll, what has the ethical idea of the common good yielded to in America?

3. According to Carroll, how might the American economy affect parents' decisions to have children?

What happens when a mainstream institution is taken over by its fringe? One answer plays itself out in the Republican Party, where lunatic rhetoric now defines politics. Another shows itself in the Catholic Church, whose leadership has fallen into the trap of single-issue moralism. That the aggressively lobbying Catholic bishops were prepared to kill the health care reform bill in the House last week [November 2009] over abortion shows how far they have come from the broad tradition of Catholic social teaching that sees the common good as involving multiple values. Negotiation and compromise are essential to solidarity. When values conflict, as they inevitably do in legislation, ethical reasoning assumes a delicate balance, weighing one issue against another. Abortion represents one such moral question that carries special gravity for Catholics. Despite the bishops' assertions, however, there are others—notably, a universal right to quality health care, which the bishops have supported for years, but which they were prepared last week to throw overboard rather than accept a compromise that would have covered abortions by patient co-payments instead of government funds.

## Common Good

Because the American Catholic drumbeat on abortion has been so loud and unrelenting in recent years, it is easy to forget that the Catholic Church has long had a complex and nuanced approach to moral questions. That is reflected in Pope Benedict's recent [2009] encyclical *Charity in Truth* [*Caritas in Veritate*], which offers timely reflections on globalization, development, the economic crisis, and threats to the environment—all based on a broadly defined "common good" that has tremendous relevance for the debate unfolding in Washington. But Benedict gives marching orders to the bishops, which came last week from a different book. His complex vision of the common good was nowhere in evidence as the health care bill was reduced to one question, defined in its most parochial terms, a dreadful narrowing of concern. Where, for example, was Catholic institutional weight early in the legislative process when undocumented immigrants were excluded from the health care benefits?

The ethical ideal of "common good" has its secular equivalent in the political idea of "commonwealth," but in America that has yielded to a new organizing image—the casino. The world is divided between the lucky few and the miserable many, with everyone agreeing that there simply isn't enough to go around. Therefore, it's me, myself, and I. Our traditional faith (evident as recently as during the civil rights movement) that a commonwealth can actually be achieved and protected has been eroded, with the Republican Party as the chief exemplar and advocate of this radical individualism. But that's not all: Our self-aggrandizing polarization is driven also by contempt for out-groups like dark-skinned newcomers, gay people, and the very poor. We know who we are by whom we hate. Alas, Catholic leaders talk like that now, too—about their opponents in debate.

Here is where the health care legislation comes in—as nothing less than an attempt to rescue some semblance of common-good politics, for the benefit of all. That is why the readiness of the Catholic bishops to sell out the reform bill was so disturbing. Single-issue politics always distorts the larger picture—and today's larger picture threatens the transformation of the commonwealth into an unjust and uncivil gambling den.

## Excerpt from Pope Benedict's Encylical *Charity in Truth*

We often reduce the self to the psyche and confuse the soul's health with emotional well-being. These oversimplifications stem from a profound failure to understand the spiritual life, and they obscure the fact that the development of individuals and peoples depends partly on the resolution of problems of a spiritual nature. *Development must include not just material growth, but also spiritual growth*, since the human person is a "unity of body and soul," born of God's creative love and destined for eternal life. The human being develops when he grows in the spirit, when his soul comes to know itself and the truths that God has implanted deep within, when he enters into dialogue with himself and his Creator. When he is far away from God, man is unsettled and ill at ease. Social and psychological alienation and the many neuroses that afflict affluent societies are attributable in part to spiritual factors. A prosperous society, highly developed in material terms but weighing heavily on the soul, is not of itself conducive to authentic development. The new forms of slavery to drugs and the lack of hope into which so many people fall can be explained not only in sociological and psychological terms, but also in essentially spiritual terms. The emptiness in which the soul feels abandoned, despite the availability of countless therapies for body and psyche, leads to suffering. *There cannot be holistic development and universal common good unless people's spiritual and moral welfare is taken into account*, considered in their totality as body and soul.

*Pope Benedict XVI, Caritas in Veritate (Charity in Truth), Libreria Editrice Vaticane, 2009. www.vatican.va.*

## Unemployment and Other Issues

Against those who argue that the U.S. Catholic bishops have no business intruding into politics as they did last week, I argue that they should be lobbying the hell out of the entire economic-recovery process. If abortion were among numerous concerns, each of which deserves attention, bishops might rise to the challenge, say, of figures that show unemployment skyrocketing among young people between 16 and 24, even as student-aid cuts are forcing them out of school. And, by the way, what will that do to pregnancy rates? How many "unwanted children," for that matter, are not actually "unwanted" at all? What if their parents have simply been made to feel, in the casino economy, that they will never have the resources to care for children? What are the bishops doing for them? Why is the U.S. Conference [of Catholic Bishops] not excoriating corporations and banks for their failure to protect jobs instead of top salaries and bonuses? Why, that is, has Catholic ethical concern been so allowed to narrow as to have become shriveled?

We hear little or nothing from Catholic leaders on such questions because, just as extreme voices have made American politics toxic, so extreme voices have poisoned the teaching authority of the Church. Slash-and-burn single-mindedness is fanatic. Hence the excluding absolutism on the abortion question. Hence the dangerous exacerbation of the worst trends in American public life. "There cannot be holistic development and universal common good," Pope Benedict warned in his encyclical, "unless people's spiritual and moral welfare is taken into account, considered in their totality as body and soul." Precisely.

# Periodical Bibliography

*The following articles have been selected to supplement the diverse views presented in this chapter.*

| | |
|---|---|
| James Carroll | "The Catholic Church's Next Scandal," Blogs & Stories, October 17, 2009. www.thedailybeast.com. |
| Dan DiLeo | "Alternatives to Condoms: The Catholic Church and Contraceptives," *Cornell Daily Sun*, March 31, 2009. http://cornellsun.com. |
| Andrew Downie | "Nine-Year-Old's Abortion Outrages Brazil's Catholic Church," *Time*, March 6, 2009. |
| Cathy Lynn Grossman | "Catholic Church Updates Code on Birth Technology," *USA Today*, December 12, 2008. |
| Deal Hudson | "Battle over Abortion Funding in Congress Pits Catholics Against Each Other," Lifenews.com, January 4, 2010. www.lifenews.com. |
| Paul S. Loverde | "Health Care Update," *Catholic Herald*, November 24, 2009. www.catholicherald.com. |
| Daniel C. Maguire | "The Moderate Roman Catholic Position on Contraception and Abortion," Religious Consultation. www.religiousconsultation. |
| National Institutes of Health | "Stem Cell Basics," April 28, 2009. http://stemcells.nih.gov. |
| Jack Nelson, as told to Kathryn Jean Lopez | "Catholic Health Care in the Age of Obama," *National Review Online*, September 22, 2009. www.nationalreview.com. |
| Frank Newport | "Catholics Similar to Mainstream on Abortion, Stem Cells," Gallup, March 30, 2009. www.gallup.com. |
| Victor L. Simpson | "Pope: Condoms Not the Answer to AIDS," *Huffington Post*, March 17, 2009. |

OPPOSING
VIEWPOINTS®
SERIES

CHAPTER 4

# How Can the Catholic Church Grow?

# Chapter Preface

In Latin America, the population traditionally has been overwhelmingly Catholic. In recent years, however, that has started to change. A Protestant movement known as Pentecostalism has grown increasingly popular throughout the region. Pentecostalism emphasizes a direct personal experience of God and includes an expressive worship style, including uttering speech-like syllables that are believed to be a holy language referred to as "speaking in tongues."

The growth of Pentecostals in Latin America has been dramatic. According to the Pew Forum on Religion & Public Life, Pentecostals accounted for only about .01 million Latin Americans in 1900; by 1970, that number had increased to 12.6 million; by 1990, to 118.6 million; and by 2005, to 156.9 million. Thus, in the last hundred years, Pentecostals have jumped from virtually 0 percent to 28.1 percent of the population of the region. Countries with particularly large Pentecostal populations include Brazil, Chile, Nicaragua, and Guatemala, the last of which has had two Pentecostal presidents. Mexico, Colombia, and Peru have much smaller Pentecostal populations, but there, too, the number of Pentecostals is on the rise.

Antonio Castillo, writing in a May 5, 2009, article on the Web site newmatilda.com, noted that the growth of Pentecostalism is "not coming primarily from population growth, migration, or indigenous religions" but "directly in disenchanted droves from the Catholic Church." According to Castillo, ten thousand people a day leave the Catholic Church in Latin America, eight thousand of whom plan to convert to Protestantism. Castillo suggests that the disenchantment with Catholicism and the growth of Pentecostalism are due, in large part, to Pentecostalism's appeal to the poor. Pentecostalism claims that "wealth is a divine blessing achieved by an active and frequent participation in the religious services," says Manuel Ossa, a theologian quoted in the article. This direct link between prosperity and religious observance is attractive to many of the poor in Latin America, Ossa argues.

The Catholic Church has tried to respond to the challenge of Pentecostalism in various ways. While he was alive, Pope John Paul II attacked the mass conversions to Pentecostalism "as an 'invasion of the sects' that is robbing Latin America of its Catholic culture and destroying its social cohesion," according to the article "Overview: Pentecostalism in Latin America" on the Pew Forum's Web site. More recently, however, the Catholic Church has responded to Pentecostalism not by denouncing it but by adopting some of its style of worship. Expressive, personal movements within the Catholic Church, referred to as charismatic movements, often include spiritual healing and speaking in tongues as part of their services, just as Pentecostal churches do. These Catholic charismatic movements have been growing quickly, and they now "claim 24 percent of Brazilians, 21 percent of Chileans, and 40 percent of Guatemalans," writes Francis X. Rocca in a May 2, 2007, article for Religion News Service.

Catholicism is changing rapidly not only in Latin America, but also in Africa, Europe, the United States, and throughout the world. The following viewpoints look at some of the most important aspects of these transformations.

"As fully-fledged Anglicans also seek refuge from liberalism in the shelter of Rome, it is feared that the proposal could deal a deadly blow to the 77 million–strong Anglican Communion."

# The Catholic Church May Gain Converts by Absorbing Disaffected Anglicans

*Ruth Gledhill, Sophie Tedmanson, Giles Whittell, and Richard Owen*

*Ruth Gledhill, Sophie Tedmanson, Giles Whittell, and Richard Owen are writers for the* Times of London. *In the following viewpoint, they report on Pope Benedict XVI's offer to allow Anglican leaders to join the Catholic Church on generous terms, including the possibility of allowing married Anglican priests to become Catholic priests. The authors suggest that this move could seriously wound the Anglican church, as priests disaffected with the ordination of women and gay bishops convert to Rome.*

As you read, consider the following questions:

1. Who is Archbishop John Hepworth?

Ruth Gledhill, Sophie Tedmanson, Giles Whittell, and Richard Owen, "400,000 Former Anglicans Worldwide Seek Immediate Unity with Rome," *Times Online*, October 22, 2009. www.timesonline.co.uk. Reproduced by permission.

2. As described in the viewpoint, when did the Church of England decide to ordain women priests, and how many priests left the church as a result?

3. According to Lawrence Cunningham, what repercussions will Pope Benedict XVI's offer have for the Catholic Church?

L eaders of more than 400,000 Anglicans who quit over women priests [the result of an ongoing controversy among Anglicans about the ordination of female and homosexual priests] are to seek immediate unity with Rome under the apostolic constitution announced by Pope Benedict XVI. They will be among the first to take up an option allowing Anglicans to join an "ordinariate" that brings them into full communion with Roman Catholics while retaining elements of their Anglican identity.

## A Blow to Anglicanism

The pope's move is regarded by some Anglicans as one of the most dramatic developments in Protestant Christendom since the Reformation gave birth to the Church of England [the first Anglican church] 400 years ago.

Archbishop John Hepworth, the twice-married Primate of the Traditional Anglican Communion, who led negotiations with the Congregation for the Doctrine of the Faith [the Catholic agency charged with overseeing doctrine] in Rome, said he was "profoundly moved" by the pope's decision and would immediately seek the approval of the group's 400,000 members worldwide to join.

He described the development as "a moment of grace, perhaps even a moment of history".

As fully-fledged Anglicans also seek refuge from liberalism in the shelter of Rome, it is feared that the proposal could deal a deadly blow to the 77 million–strong Anglican Communion, which already faces schism over homosexual ordination.

Up to 500 members of Forward in Faith, the traditionalist grouping that opposes women bishops, are meeting this weekend [October 2009] to debate the pope's offer of a home for former Anglican laity and married priests.

Many are waiting for the publication of a code of practice by Rome to flesh out what is on offer before deciding whether to go.

Insiders believe that Rome's new canonical solution to the Anglican crisis could tempt entire dioceses and possibly even a province.[1]

More than 440 clergy took compensation [a financial payment] and left the Church of England, most for Rome, after the General Synod voted to ordain women priests in 1992. More than 30 returned.

## An Attractive Offer

The pope has made it significantly more attractive for Anglicans to move over this time by offering a universal solution that allows them to retain crucial aspects of their identity and to set up seminaries that will, presumably, train married men for the Catholic priesthood. But any serving clergyman would face a marked loss of income. A job as a clergyman in the Church of England comes with a stipend of £22,250 and free accommodation. Catholic priests earn about £8,000, paid by their parish and topped up by a diocese where the parish cannot afford even that.

The archbishop of Canterbury, Dr Rowan Williams, indicated that there would be no compensation this time. It was only introduced at the last minute previously as a way of get-

1. The Anglican Communion is divided into thirty-eight national or multinational provinces and smaller dioceses within each province.

## Female Ordination in the Anglican Church

There has historically been a threefold ministry in the [Anglican] church, consisting of deacons, priests and bishops. Prior to the mid-20th century, all provinces in the Anglican Communion had refused to consider female candidates as eligible for ordination to the priesthood, no matter what their qualifications. There was little discussion on the matter. However, in the 1960s, the evolving feminist movement began to have an impact on the Anglican Communion, particularly in the developed world. Discussions of the unthinkable began. By 1974, the first female priests were ordained in the U.S. By 1998, debate had been confined to the sizeable minority of provinces which still banned the ordination of women. However, progress has not been uniform. Even in 2008, the Church in Wales refused to allow female ordination.

*Bruce A. Robinson,*
*"Ordination of Female Priests and Bishops*
*in the Worldwide Anglican Communion,"*
*ReligiousTolerance.org, May 29, 2008.*
*www.religioustolerance.org.*

ting the whole women's ordination package through the General Synod with the necessary two-thirds majorities.

Dr Michael Nazir-Ali, the former Catholic who retired this year as the Anglican bishop of Rochester, welcomed Rome's "generosity of spirit" in its recognition of Anglican patrimony. But he made clear that many issues needed to be resolved before decisions could be made. The two "flying bishops" appointed by the archbishop of Canterbury to care for opponents of women priests also said that this was not a time for "sudden decisions".

Andrew Burnham, the bishop of Ebbsfleet, and Keith Newton, the bishop of Richborough, who went last year to Rome to begin talks with the Congregation for the Doctrine of the Faith said: "Anglicans in the Catholic tradition understandably will want to stay within the Anglican Communion. Others will wish to make individual arrangements as their conscience directs. A further group will begin to form a caravan, rather like the People of Israel crossing the desert in search of the Promised Land." In the US a writer for the Jesuit magazine *America* expressed fears that some newcomers would be "nostalgists, antifeminists and antigay bigots".

At Notre Dame University in Indiana, scholars forecast a migration of Catholics into the new Anglican Catholic rite because of the sudden freedom to marry that it would grant. Professor Lawrence Cunningham called the Vatican's move a "stunning" endorsement of the married priesthood, adding that it would have immediate repercussions for Catholics. It would "raise anew the question, 'If they can do it, why can't the priests of Rome?'"

Archbishop Robert Duncan, of the Anglican Church in North America, which broke away from the Episcopal Church over the ordination of the gay Gene Robinson as the bishop of New Hampshire, said: "We rejoice that the Holy See has opened this doorway, which represents another step in the co-operation and relationship between our churches."

In Rome, Vittorio Messori, who has cowritten books with the pope, said that the Anglican Communion was already losing followers because of female and gay priests. "More Muslims go to the mosques in London than Anglicans go to church," he said. "The exit of half a million Anglicans to Rome will only confirm a trend."

> "Allowing married former Anglican clergy to serve as married Catholic priests is sure to modify Catholics' perception of what a Catholic priest needs to be."

# Absorbing Anglicans into the Catholic Church May Have Unintended Consequences

*Gerald Floyd*

*Gerald Floyd is an American theologian who writes for the blog Creative Advance. In the following viewpoint, he argues that Pope Benedict XVI's efforts to bring disaffected Anglicans into the Catholic communion may have unintended consequences. For example, conservative Anglicans becoming Catholic may strengthen Anglican liberalism. In addition, allowing converted Anglican priests to remain married may increase pressure for married Catholic priests. Finally, Floyd suggests that if women Anglican priests want to convert, the desire to accommodate them might result in a push for female Catholic priests.*

Gerald Floyd, "Rome Absorbing Anglicans: Unintended Consequences for Both Communions?" Creative Advance, October 22, 2009. Reproduced by permission. http://creativeadvance.blogspot.com.

As you read, consider the following questions:

1. According to Floyd, what news outlets carried the news of the pope's offer to Anglicans?

2. According to the Roman Catholic Church, what Anglican practices had led some Anglican priests to want to convert to Rome?

3. According to Cardinal William Levada, the Catholic Church is planning to allow married Anglicans into the priesthood only under what circumstances?

Multiple outlets are carrying the news that the Vatican is planning to create new church structures that would absorb disaffected Anglicans but allow them to retain their distinctive liturgy and spiritual practices, including at least some married priests. The outlets include the *National Catholic Reporter*, CNN, *USA Today*, the Associated Press, and the *Toronto Star*.

## Anglicans in Turmoil

The news was most unsettling in London. There the *Times* has run several articles about it in the last two days, including two in banner headlines at the top of its front page, along with numerous commentaries.

Wednesday's [October 2009] front page screamed "Papal gambit stuns Church" and included the picture of a very distraught-looking archbishop of Canterbury in the middle of the page. The online version was entitled "Pope's gambit could see 1,000 quit Church of England." It suggested as many as 1,000 priests could leave the Church of England [the first Anglican church], and perhaps thousands more from Anglican churches in Australia and America. It said Pope Benedict's planned decree "is a serious blow to attempts by the archbishop of Canterbury, Dr. Rowan Williams, to save the Anglican Communion from further fragmentation and threatens to

wreck decades of ecumenical dialogue." The *Times* character-
ized Dr. Williams at a joint press conference with the Catholic
archbishop of Westminster as "uncomfortable," and said that
in a letter to Anglican bishops and clergy Williams acknowl-
edged being blindsided.

A related article published online the night before said
"Vatican moves to poach traditional Anglicans." The *Times*
said the Vatican made its decisions after secret negotiations in
Rome with at least six traditionalist Anglican bishops and
with no direct discussion with the archbishop of Canterbury—
not alerting him to the radical nature of the changes until two
weeks ago, not giving him formal notice until last weekend,
and basically roping him into a hastily called joint press conference with the archbishop of Westminster.

Thursday's front page had a huge picture of Pope Benedict
under a headline that read, "When in Rome: 400,000 Anglicans plan to convert." The online version was entitled, "400,000
former Anglicans worldwide seek immediate union with
Rome." It reported: "Archbishop John Hepworth, the twice-
married Primate of the Traditional Anglican Communion,
who led negotiations with the Congregation for the Doctrine
of the Faith in Rome, said he was 'profoundly moved' by the
pope's decision and would immediately seek the approval of
the group's 400,000 members worldwide to join."

## Long-Term Consequences

Obviously the move is a big deal for the Anglican Communion—and perhaps Rome's most effective challenge to the
Church of England in the 450 years since Henry VIII.[1] But it
is important for both communions to recognize that the papal
initiative may have several unintended consequences for
Catholics as well as Anglicans—consequences that may prove
far more significant and even more enduring than whatever
Benedict may gain in the short term.

1. The Anglican church was formed in 1534 when Henry VIII separated the Church of
England from the Roman Catholic Church.

The official Vatican announcement, made October 20, 2009, portrays Rome's move as a pastoral response to Anglicans who are distressed about specific recent developments in their communion and who "have declared that they share the common Catholic faith as it is expressed in the *Catechism of the Catholic Church* and accept the Petrine ministry as something Christ willed for the Church." The announcement added: "At the same time, they have told us of the importance of their Anglican traditions of spirituality and worship for their faith journey." Evidently the Vatican considered accommodating the latter a small price to pay for gaining these Anglicans' adherence to official church teaching.

The document is not coy about which Anglican developments caused the distress Rome wants to relieve: "In the years since the Council, some Anglicans have abandoned the tradition of conferring Holy Orders only on men by calling women to the priesthood and the episcopacy. More recently, some segments of the Anglican Communion have departed from the common biblical teaching on human sexuality . . . by the ordination of openly homosexual clergy and the blessing of homosexual partnerships." The immediate impact of absorbing Anglicans who cannot abide these positions will be to increase the ranks of Catholics who support the Roman alternatives.

Those are the intended consequences, at any rate. Yet other consequences can be envisioned which Rome clearly does not intend.

## Liberal Anglicans Strengthened

One is that it will strengthen the more liberal position of those who remain in the Anglican Communion, not only in the Church of England but also in Canada and in the Episcopal Church USA [the American branch of the Anglican Communion]. Rowan Williams may end up presiding over a considerably smaller Anglican Communion, but it will be

## The Pope's Initiative May Strengthen Anglican Tolerance

The pope's [Pope Benedict XVI's] initiative [to allow Anglicans into the full communion of the Catholic Church] could serve to move the Church of England in a mysterious way. It could concentrate all our minds on what it means to be a tolerant, broad church in the Reformist tradition. An unintended consequence of the pope's offer could be the recognition of a rich tradition that can accommodate all kinds of churchmanship. And, crucially, all kinds of people on equal terms, whatever their sexuality or gender.

*George Pitcher,*
*"Sex Is a Stumbling Block for Anglicans on the Road to Rome,"*
Telegraph, *October 26, 2009. www.telegraph.co.uk.*

comprised of Christians who are firmly committed to changes they believe God's Spirit has inspired. They will no longer feel the drag of those who believe otherwise.

The *Times* of London articles already speculate that it will accelerate the ordination of female bishops in the Church of England, which had been on hold in deference to those who already disapproved of female priests. It should also strengthen the existing practice in the United States. It will also embolden bishops and national Anglican churches who strongly believe that blessing same-sex unions is an important matter of justice and equal treatment of baptized Christians.

It should also strengthen those in other Protestant denominations that have adopted the controverted Anglican practices, such as the Evangelical Lutheran Church in America, which in August decided to accept noncelibate clergy members and lay leaders who are in "lifelong" and "monogamous" same-sex relationships. Bilateral agreements between American Lutherans and Episcopalians will take on new importance and additional ones would become more likely.

By allowing married Anglican priests to serve as Catholic priests in its new Anglican ordinariates, Rome's move may actually strengthen the tradition of married clergy in the Anglican Communion. The message Rome is conveying, after all, is that Christians have found some value in married clergy. How can this not increase the commitment to married clergy among Anglicans who remain?

It should also give new impetus to their objection to Rome's earlier [1896] declaration that Anglican orders are "null and void." The Anglican clergy have long held that Rome's position was historically inaccurate in the first place, that it was eclipsed by subsequent events, and that even prominent Catholic bishops no longer consider it appropriate. Even though the Vatican is insisting on re-ordination of the Anglican clergy before they can function as Catholic priests, the fact that this apparently will be done with ease and with no additional doctrinal formation will tend to reinforce the Anglican position that their priests and bishops have always been validly ordained.

## Impact on Celibacy

It may also impact the celibacy policy of the Roman [Catholic] Church itself. The Vatican is at pains to distinguish the status of married Anglican clergy who now wish to profess allegiance to Rome from Catholic priests who vowed celibacy and then married. But allowing married former Anglican clergy to serve as married Catholic priests is sure to modify Catholics' perception of what a Catholic priest needs to be, and to highlight that celibacy is a policy choice and not the unchangeable essence of the priesthood.

The Vatican announcement implied that seminarians trained for the Anglican ordinariates would continue to be allowed to marry. However, an article today from Religion News Service waffles on that: "Cardinal William Levada, head of the Vatican's doctrinal office, suggested on Tuesday [October 20, 2009] that the new diocese will not ordain married men unless they have already started their preparation in Anglican seminaries, or permit unmarried priests to take wives after ordination." The article implies that if the Vatican does not make provision for a permanent married priesthood in the Anglican ordinariates, it will be a deal breaker for some Anglicans. But even allowing existing seminarians to marry before ordination means that Rome will face pressure to allow more marriages when new seminarians are recruited for the Anglican structures.

A scenario that could result from Rome's new policy would place Rome in an interesting quandary. It is unlikely but not unthinkable that there are female Anglican priests who (obviously) favor ordination of women but not ordination of gay people or the blessing of same-sex unions. If such a female priest were to apply for admission as a Catholic priest, Rome would not be able to accept her because of its position that ordaining women is impossible. Yet Rome would be turning down an Anglican who professes everything else required by the *Catechism of the Catholic Church*. It would also face pressure from Catholic women who would regard the Anglican female priest as the embodiment of what is indeed possible in the Catholic Church. Clearly the Vatican does not intend by this initiative to strengthen the women's ordination movement in Catholicism. But that result may not be avoidable.

Nearly everyone will agree that Pope Benedict's gambit is a game changer for Anglican-Catholic relations. But what Benedict wants may not be what Benedict gets. There are other players with other agendas in both communions and in the other Christian churches. It will be interesting to see if Benedict has outmaneuvered them, or just outwitted himself.

> "Fortunately, along came John Paul II
> who made the Church stricter. The
> Catholic Church started to grow again."

# The Catholic Church Needs to Be Stricter to Grow

## Christopher Chantrill

*Christopher Chantrill writes for the* American Thinker *and blogs at www.roadtothemiddleclass.com. In the following viewpoint, he argues that churches tend to be most popular when they are moderately strict, imposing some religious costs on members and staying at least somewhat distinct from secular society. Chantrill believes that in the 1960s, the Catholic Church became too moderate and therefore began to lose members. He praises Pope John Paul II for making the Church stricter and more attractive.*

As you read, consider the following questions:

1. According to Chantrill, who is Matthew Parris and how does he want the Catholic Church to change?

2. According to Chantrill, what is the difference between Jehovah's Witnesses and Unitarian Universalists in terms of their distance from secular society?

Christopher Chantrill, "Unsolicited Advice for the Church," *American Thinker*, April 11, 2005. Reproduced by permission of the publisher and the author.

3. As cited by the author, when did the Catholic Church reduce its tension with the rest of society?

Ever since the death of [Pope] John Paul II [in 2005], people have been generously offering to help plan the future of the Catholic Church. They recognize that the Church occupies a unique position in the world, and they want it to succeed. [Snort, cough, giggle.]

Okay, they just want to graft their own agenda onto the Church's robust root stock and grow their own fruit upon it.

The British atheist Matthew Parris wants the Church to become amiably feeble like the Church of England, and the Left wants it to incorporate its secular sacraments of abortion, women in the priesthood, contraception, condoms, and gay marriage into the already substantial list of seven sacraments: baptism, confirmation, eucharist, penance and reconciliation, anointing of the sick, holy orders, and matrimony.

## Marketing the Church

All this free advice would be comical if it weren't so outrageous. How in the world does a secular journalist imagine that she has standing to advise the Conclave of the College of Cardinals on the content of the Catholic faith? Strictly speaking, of course, nobody has standing, since the Church has always been a top-down church, a *magisterium*. If you prefer bottom-up religion, Protestant churches offer a different approach.

But there is one way in which we interfering opiners can help. We can apply our Yankee ingenuity to the market share issue. It may seem sacrilegious to apply the crass reasoning of the marketplace to the godly realm of religion. But churches are also institutions which rely on economic inputs to maintain their activities. The Catholic Church is the oldest organization in the world, and it has survived this long by being both spiritual and pragmatic, though the two imperatives are often in tension.

Assume for the sake of discussion that the Catholic Church wants to remain the market leader in the global religion industry: What should it do to stay No. 1?

The U.S. is home to a coterie of academic sociologists that has studied just this problem: How does a church find the 'sweet spot' in the religious market, and grow to become market leader? That is what sociologist Rodney Stark and his collaborators have done.

Suppose you think in terms of supply and demand for religion, and symbolize religious organizations as 'religious firms' led by 'religious entrepreneurs.' What then? You could think of a big, corporate religious firm as a 'church,' and a start-up religious firm as a 'sect' or 'cult.'

The whole point of a church, as Will Herberg advised in 1966, is to take its stand 'against the spirit of the age—because the world and the age are always, to a degree, to an important degree, in rebellion against God.' There should be, and there usually is, a 'tension' between a church and society. A church should keep a certain distance from the secular world to demonstrate the distance between what is and what should be.

Some religious firms, such as the Jehovah's Witnesses, keep a large distance from the secular world, maintaining a separate community in 'high tension' with secular society. Sects usually impose heavy costs and prohibitions upon their members. Others, like the average Pentecostal or 'fundamentalist' church, maintain a medium tension with godless, secular society and impose fewer costs and prohibitions upon their members. There are others, liberal religious firms like the Unitarian Universalist Church, that maintain almost no tension with the dominant secular society and the educated, secular elite. For their members there is almost no cost to membership.

Church members usually understand that to get a really superior product you have to pay more.

For budding religious entrepreneurs or CEOs [chief executive officers], the question arises: Is there a 'best' level of tension? In [the book] *Acts of Faith*, Rodney Stark and Roger Finke asked just this question, and they found that there is a bell curve associated with religious tension or strictness. Very strict and very liberal churches are usually small. The 'sweet spot' with the biggest churches is the moderately strict religious market niche in moderate tension with secular society.

## Stricter Means Bigger

The Catholic Church used to have a reputation for strictness. It was a church that was notorious (or renowned, depending on your perspective) for imposing substantial costs upon its adherents, in particular upon its clergy, the male celibate priests and female celibate nuns. But in the 1960s the Catholic Church suddenly decided to reduce its tension with the rest of society, and 'updated' its doctrines and its beliefs. It reduced the cost of being a Catholic (by relaxing the threat of excommunication, the requirements to attend church, and meatless Fridays) and it reduced the benefit of being a religious priest or nun (mainly by annihilating the feeling of being set apart, according to Stark, 'in a special state of holiness'). All of a sudden, the churches started to empty and some of the religiously inclined lost their vocations.

Fortunately, along came John Paul II who made the Church stricter. The Catholic Church started to grow again except, of course, in Old Europe.

You can understand what the unpaid, unsolicited secular advisers are proposing for the Catholic Church. They are proposing that it reduce its 'tension' with secular society. They are proposing that it become smaller.

"What once was a European-ethnic church will become a predominantly Hispanic and Third World immigrant church."

# The Catholic Church and Other Religious Groups Will Experience Demographic Changes

*Sean Scallon*

*Sean Scallon is a writer and journalist who writes the blog Beating the Powers That Be. In the following viewpoint, he argues that the Catholic Church will change demographically as Hispanic immigrants become a majority of the parishioners. As a result, he maintains, ethnic Europeans will leave the Catholic Church to join Orthodox churches. Scallon also believes that Islam in the United States will grow thanks to Muslim immigrants and an increasing number of white converts dissatisfied with Christianity.*

As you read, consider the following questions:

1. According to Scallon, why will the Catholic Church not oppose immigration?

2. As explained by Scallon, what Orthodox church could absorb most American converts?

3. What aspects of Islam does Scallon believe might appeal to right-wingers?

Demographics is destiny and that's true not just in politics but business, education, sports, entertainment, culture and religion.

Especially religion.

That's because numbers and numbers of adherents determine whether or not your faith is taken seriously or is just another kooky cult.

There are two demographic trends that may occur in the 21st century inside the U.S. that could alter several faiths in the process. Those trends are from Catholic to Orthodox and from (nominal) Christian to Islam.

## Catholicism and Demographics

We start with the Catholic Church. It's no secret the U.S. Catholic Church is in a deep crisis. The numerous sexual molestation scandals[1] and the class action lawsuits that have followed are draining diocesan treasuries dry. Many such dioceses are selling off buildings like closed churches and schools and other real estate properties they own. On top of that, the shortage of priests and nuns in the U.S. means more such closures are on the way. And because of that shortage, the Church's institutions, its colleges, hospitals and other charitable foundations, will become completely secularized within the next 20 years. The whole infrastructure of the Church within the U.S. could be almost gone within that time period.

1. Starting in about 2001, it was revealed that numerous Catholic priests had molested young boys, and that the Church hierarchy covered up these acts.

The U.S. Catholic Church will survive however. It has faced worse challenges in its history and has always survived. But to survive means to adapt and adapting means change and the U.S. Catholic Church will be transformed by this process. The transformation will come demographically as what once was a European-ethnic church will become a predominantly Hispanic and Third World immigrant church.

This is also a process that's going on worldwide as well. Philip Jenkins, the Penn State University theology professor and writer for *Chronicles*, has documented this coming transformation of the Christian world thanks to demographics in numerous articles and books. Numbers mean power and such power within the Church will come from its Third World adherents. There's no doubt [the] next pope will probably be from the Third World, perhaps Latin or South America first (with a bishop of European immigrant descent) followed by an African pope after that. We've already seen the Third World's power within the Anglican community. Several Episcopal churches in the U.S. have left their local dioceses in schisms to align themselves with Anglican dioceses in Third World locations because their bishops are more traditional than their Western counterparts, who are ordaining women and homosexual bishops.

What is fueling the change in the U.S. Catholic Church is immigration. More Hispanic immigrants and other Catholic immigrants from the Third World are filling the pews and in many cases what were once empty pews, especially in big cities. Now as immigration spreads from big cities and the coasts to small towns in the Midwest and South, such change will take place in churches in these locations as well. It's the Catholic Church that will absorb most of the new immigrants. Although a good chunk of Hispanic immigrants are Pentecostals, they tend to form their own churches separately. Hispanic Catholics are moving into existing communities and existing churches.

## Changes in Ethnic Communities

All this leaves the European ethnic in a quandary. The term "Catholic" means universal and as such it should not matter what race or ethnic group anyone who calls themselves Catholic is. All are welcomed. Yet such churches were the anchors of previous ethnic communities. Such change can be quite jarring, especially when you add it onto change within the neighborhood, change in the business community and change within the schools thanks to unlimited immigration. It doesn't take long for one Hispanic mass to become all masses at some point.

Because of this change, some European-ethnic Catholics wish that the bishops would either take a stand against immigration or [at] least not be noisy promoters of it like Los Angeles Archbishop Roger Mahony. Unfortunately they are whistling past the graveyard. Not even the most conservative of bishops, like Omaha's [Fabian] Bruskewitz, are going to oppose unlimited immigration nor will any be recalled by Rome for such support like Mahony. The Catholic Church in the U.S. is an immigrant church. Always has been. Always will be. To its bishops and administrators, seeing one immigrant group coming into the Church and overtaking another is simply the natural wave of history. It would be unthinkable of them to turn [and] oppose immigration, especially when such immigrants and their money are going to be ones to keep the Church afloat during its time of transformation. Opponents of unlimited immigration must understand that is how the Church thinks and operates and it perfectly fits with its history. It [is] not a "Popish"[2] plot to undermine the United States. This writer (and Catholic) nearly deleted VDARE.com from his list of favorite Web sites last year because some of its writers began waving the bloody shirt of "rum, Romanism

---

2. "Popish" is sometimes used as an insult against Catholics, especially historically in England.

## Hispanics in the United States

Hispanics are the largest and youngest minority group in the United States. One in five schoolchildren is Hispanic. One in four newborns is Hispanic. Never before in this country's history has a minority ethnic group made up so large a share of the youngest Americans. By force of numbers alone, the kinds of adults these young Latinos become will help shape the kind of society America becomes in the 21st century.

*Pew Hispanic Center, "Between Two Worlds: How Young Latinos Come of Age in America," December 11, 2009. http://pewhispanic.org.*

and rebellion" until Peter Brimelow[3] thankfully set them straight and also pointed out Protestantism's many contributions to our nation's immigration problems.

But again the quandary for [the] European-ethnic Catholic remains. His numbers have been reduced by intermarriage, by the destruction of ethnic neighborhoods by urban renewal and the interstate highway system, by suburban sprawl, by the Church's own problems and divisions within it and by his or her own laziness and sloth. If you don't show up for mass or to volunteer or be a part of the community, you will lose power and influence to those who do. Whoever said that life is all about showing up was dead on in this regard. So what to do? Join the Orthodox Church.

## Rise of the Orthodox Church

The Orthodox Church has a number of appeals to the European-ethnic Catholic. It is a church that is ethnically con-

3. VDARE.com is an anti-immigration Web site supported by *Forbes* editor Peter Brimelow.

scious and fuses the idea of the church to that of the nation and the culture. That's why there are Greek Orthodox churches, Russian Orthodox churches, Romanian Orthodox churches and so forth. (Only the Polish Catholic Church and Uniate churches [Catholic churches in Eastern Europe] loyal to Rome are that way amongst Catholics). It is a decentralized church, which means its doctrines and practices of worship are not subject to the whims of a whole Vatican Council. It's a church that has avoided a lot of the doctrinal disputes that have divided the Catholic churches because it stays true to its traditions and doctrines which it traces back to the original Christian church. Its mass has gone unchanged for many centuries and one doesn't have to worry about whether the new priest is going to allow guitars and drums during the worship service, disallow bells or kneeling or whatever fashion of mass is in vogue from the seminary. It's a church whose priests are married which means the problems the Catholic Church has had with homosexual priests (the ones that don't take their vows of celibacy seriously anyway) aren't a problem with the Orthodox. It is the Orthodox that is going to be more suspicious of mass immigration (especially immigration from Islamic nations) than other religions.

Of course, if you are an Irish, Italian, French or German Catholic, you just can't pop into [the] Serbian Orthodox Church and say "I'm a new convert!" unless you marry a Serb. It just doesn't work that way. To solve that problem, the Orthodox Church of America (OCA) exists. Formed in the early 1970s by the Russian Patriarchy and separate from it, the OCA is an Americanized version of the Russian Church with its services in English and with pews and so forth. Many of the churches are old Russian ones like Holy Trinity, but the OCA also incorporates other ethnic groups like Albanian and Romanian Orthodox that never had separate ethnic bishoprics like the Greeks or Serbs do. The OCA could very easily incorporate ethnic European Catholic refugees in their own

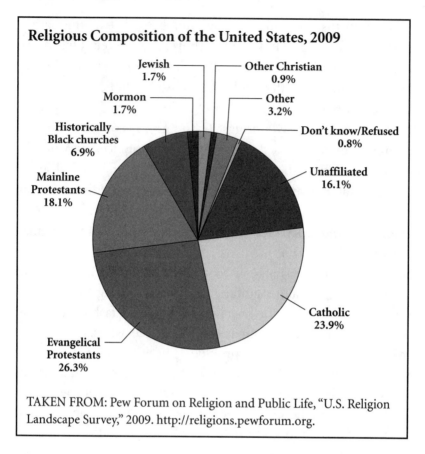

**Religious Composition of the United States, 2009**

Jewish 1.7%

Other Christian 0.9%

Mormon 1.7%

Other 3.2%

Historically Black churches 6.9%

Don't know/Refused 0.8%

Mainline Protestants 18.1%

Unaffiliated 16.1%

Catholic 23.9%

Evangelical Protestants 26.3%

TAKEN FROM: Pew Forum on Religion and Public Life, "U.S. Religion Landscape Survey," 2009. http://religions.pewforum.org.

churches. Right now the OCA has over 100 churches and a million members, slow but steady growth that I think could easily accelerate in the 21st century. Conservative writer Rod Dreher of Crunchy Con [blog] fame has already made the switch from Catholicism to Eastern Orthodoxy and I think others will too.

## Conversion to Islam

The other trend that will take place will be those from nominal Christian backgrounds converting to Islam. Such conversions have taken place among African Americans for [a] long time and famous ones like [basketball player] Lew Alcindor to Kareem Abdul-Jabbar and [boxer] Cassius Clay to Muhammad Ali. The Nation of Islam [NOI], an organization of Black Muslims, has dominated the Islamic discourse within [the] U.S. for many years. However, the NOI's racist rhetoric against whites has kept Islam's numbers in the U.S. down from what they could potentially be.

This will change too in the 21st century. Growth in Islam will come from Third World immigration of course. But it will also come from white converts as well, and they will come from two sources of thought.

Islam always has had an ideological appeal to those on the far Left and Right. To a cultural Marxist, Islam is the god that hasn't failed (unlike communism), at least not yet. Its diverse, multicultural following and the fact that it is the religion of the Third Word, i.e., it was founded there and expanded there outside of Europe and the West, makes it a perfect vehicle for cultural upheaval and egalitarianism. Marxism derided religion which limited its appeal while Islam is a religion and has mass appeal. And within an adversarial culture, converting to Islam becomes the perfect vehicle to shock one's parents and friends and peers. Indeed, [French philosopher] Jean-Paul Sartre himself became more and more fascinated with Islam as the Communist Left declined in his later years. This has more chance of happening with the nominal baptized or secular Christian than anyone else. Think of John Walker Lindh, the Marin County, California, teenager who got fed up with [the] empty secularist lifestyle of [his] parents and neighbors and converted to Islam and joined the Taliban [a radical Islamic group] in Afghanistan, and you'll understand the type. Since 9-11 [September 11, 2001, the date of the terrorist attacks on the United States] and since George Bush II [referring to President George W. Bush, son of George H.W. Bush] gave Islam his stamp of approval by calling it a "religion of peace," there's been a growing study of Islam within the media and with others who are curious to know more about it. Such study, no doubt, will increase the size of the pool of converts for Islam within the U.S.

On the other side, Nazis have always appreciated Islam's marshal spirit and ascetic, non-bourgeois lifestyle along with its ability to submit the will of the mass towards one deity or person. They found it far superior to Christian piety which they found to be nothing more than religion for wimps, not the supermen they were supposed to be. Those who are not inclined towards Nazism still find these same qualities admirable, along with Islam's male-dominated patriarchy. Women and men do not pray together. If you are a fellow who is unchurched right at the moment because you think the modern church in the U.S. is too female dominated and has no place for you, then Islam may be your scene. Think of [a] guy who used to attend Promise Keepers [conservative Christian organization for men] rallies in football stadiums and spent his time crying on the shoulder of another guy while being told what an awful person he was. When he realized the whole thing was nothing more than a religious version of 1990s male bonding without the tom-tom drums, campfires and war paint, and when he realized his wife and her friends were laughing their heads off at him down at the salon, then you'll know the kind of person I'm talking about. In fact the crisis of the maleless church has become such a concern that, according to religious news reports, certain pastors have gotten to the point of parking Harley-Davidson motorcycles out front of the entryways of their churches and putting on football uniforms and using football metaphors to attract males back into the pews again. But Islam's call may be more enticing than that. . . .

Islam and Eastern Orthodoxy have never played major roles within the cultural, political or economic milieus of the United States largely because their numbers have never been large enough to do so, let alone attract any attention. But in this century, that could change as numbers and demography head in both faiths' direction.

*"Projecting forward to the year 2025, only one Catholic in five in the world will be a non-Hispanic Caucasian. This is the most rapid, and most sweeping, demographic transformation of Roman Catholicism in its two-thousand-year history."*

# The Catholic Church Will Grow Worldwide by Becoming Less Centered in Europe

*John L. Allen Jr.*

*John L. Allen Jr. is the Vatican correspondent for the* National Catholic Reporter *and a Vatican analyst for CNN and National Public Radio. In the following viewpoint, he argues that by 2050 the Catholic Church will have experienced massive growth in the South and shrinkage in the North. He argues that this will shift the demographic balance of the Church from Europe and North America to Latin America and Africa. Allen identifies several reasons for this trend, including worldwide population growth trends and a Catholic movement since the 1960s to allow local churches more control over their own affairs and growth.*

As you read, consider the following questions:

1. According to Allen, in 1900 how many Catholics were there in the world, and how were they distributed?

2. According to Allen's projections, in 2050 which ten countries in the world will have the largest Catholic populations?

3. According to Allen, why does Catholicism have an edge over Islam in some parts of Africa?

## The Numbers

A professor of mine once said he could write a history of the world in one sentence: "First the Agricultural Revolution happened, then the Industrial Revolution." In his estimation, those were the two historical forces with greatest consequence for shaping the modern world. Similarly, if I were asked to offer a history of Roman Catholicism in the twentieth century in one sentence, I would reply: "The center of gravity shifted from North to South." It would be a counterintuitive claim, since historians are accustomed to thinking of the great Catholic turning points of the past hundred years as the signing of the Lateran Pacts in 1929, resolving the famous "Roman question"; the pontificate of Pius XII from 1939 to 1958, which saw the Church through the Second World War and left controversy about the Church's reaction to the Holocaust; the Second Vatican Council, which launched an era of reform; and the pontificate of John Paul II (1978–2005), which exercised an enormous impact on the political and cultural debates of his day. All were indeed mammoth chapters in twentieth-century Church history. Yet in terms of both scope and scale, the eruption of the South towers over them all.

According to the invaluable work *Global Catholicism: Portrait of a World Church* by Bryan Froehle and Mary L. Gautier, in 1900, at the dawn of the twentieth century, there were roughly 266.5 million Catholics in the world, of whom over

200 million were in Europe and North America and just 66 million were scattered across the entire rest of the planet. Most of this remainder was in Latin America, some 53 million. The cultural and ethnic profile of the Church in 1900 was not terribly different from what it had been during the Council of Trent in the sixteenth century.

In 2000, by way of contrast, there were slightly under 1.1 billion Roman Catholics in the world, of whom just 350 million were Europeans and North Americans. The overwhelming majority, a staggering 720 million people, lived in Latin America, Africa, and Asia. Almost half the Catholic total, over 400 million people, lived in Latin America alone. Projecting forward to the year 2025, only one Catholic in five in the world will be a non-Hispanic Caucasian. This is the most rapid, and most sweeping, demographic transformation of Roman Catholicism in its two-thousand-year history.

These demographic trends are changing the Catholic map of the world. In the year 2000, these were the ten largest Catholic populations by country:

1. Brazil: 149 million

2. Mexico: 92 million

3. United States: 67 million

4. Philippines: 65 million

5. Italy: 56 million

6. France: 46 million

7. Colombia: 38 million

8. Spain: 38 million

9. Poland: 37 million

10. Argentina: 34 million

It's an arresting exercise to look down the line to the year 2050, drawing on population projections from the United Nations Population Division, and presuming that the Catholic percentage in each nation will remain more or less the same. This may overestimate the Catholic population in Latin America, where Catholicism is losing members both to Pentecostalism and to religious indifference, and in Europe, where secularization continues to eat away at Catholic faith and practice. It almost certainly underestimates the African totals, where growth in Catholicism is outpacing overall population growth. Nevertheless, based on the UN projections, here is the projected list of largest Catholic nations in 2050:

1. Brazil: 215 million

2. Mexico: 132 million

3. Philippines: 105 million

4. United States: 99 million

5. Democratic Republic of the Congo: 97 million

6. Uganda: 56 million

7. France: 49 million

8. Italy: 49 million

9. Nigeria: 47 million

10. Argentina: 46.1 million

For the first time, three African nations—the Democratic Republic of the Congo, Uganda, and Nigeria—will take their place among the largest Catholic nations in the world. Among the traditional Catholic powers these new African behemoths will dislodge are Spain and Poland, two cornerstones of the old European Christendom. Seven of the ten largest Catholic nations in the world will be south of the United States and Europe.

Africa offers the most striking illustration of what's happened in the past hundred years. During the twentieth century, the Catholic population of sub-Saharan Africa went from 1.9 million to more than 130 million—a staggering growth rate of 6,708 percent. Vocations are also booming. Bigard Memorial Seminary in southeastern Nigeria, with an enrollment of over 1,100, is said to be the largest Catholic seminary in the world. Its student population by itself is roughly one-fifth the total number of seminarians in the United States. Yet despite this phenomenal harvest, there is no surplus of priests in Africa, in large part because Africans are being baptized even more rapidly than they're being ordained.

Asia too saw impressive Catholic growth. Catholicism started the century as 1.2 percent of the Asian population, according to World Christian Database, and ended the century at 3 percent, meaning that the Church more than doubled its "market share." India's Catholic population grew from under 2 million to over 17 million, and should be at least 26 million by mid-century. From 1985 to 2005, the percentage of the population in South Korea which identifies itself as Catholic more than doubled, standing today at just over 11 percent, according to the 2005 census, meaning more than 5 million people. In 2000, there were more Catholic baptisms in the Philippines alone than in France, Spain, Italy, and Poland combined. In terms of Christianity as a whole, there were 350 million Christians in Asia in 2007 as compared to 372 million Buddhists. By 2010, there should be more Christians in Asia than Buddhists—a mind-bending reversal of normal impressions about the continent's preferred religion.

What all this means is that the global story of Catholicism today is growth, not decline. That's generally not the impression one picks up from casual conversation or TV sound bites in Europe or the United States, where talk of a "crisis" is the more usual fare. In 2003, David Brooks published an article in the *Atlantic Monthly* documenting global Christian expansion.

Brooks was biting in his indictment of secular elites such as those who edit the magazine for which he was writing: "A great Niagara of religious fervor is cascading down around them" he wrote, "while they stand obtuse and dry in the little cave of their own parochialism."

Numerical growth by itself, of course, does not mean that everything in the Church is hunky-dory. As Pope Benedict XVI said in July 2007, "Statistics are not our divinity." Nevertheless, the remarkable Catholic Niagara of the twentieth century does suggest a baseline of vitality in the Church that too often escapes attention amid perceptions of drift and decline in Europe and other zones of the West.

## The Causes of Catholic Growth

Peter Berger, a distinguished sociologist of religion, says that no important social phenomenon ever has just a single cause. That's certainly the case with the growth of Catholicism across the global South in the twentieth century. Believers, of course, interpret what happened as a work of the Holy Spirit. Church leaders also point to the hard work of Catholic missionaries at the retail level. Without negating the role of divine providence and direct missionary effort, social scientists also point to at least four other empirical factors: overall population growth; the transition from missionary to local churches; local circumstances that drove religious realignments; and the capacity of Christianity to embrace indigenous cultures.

*1. Population Growth.* The twentieth century witnessed a population explosion across Africa, Asia, and Latin America, and Catholicism was one of the boats lifted highest by this tide. Global demographics are therefore the single most important factor in explaining the expansion of the Catholic population in the last century. Overall, the global population went from 2.5 billion in 1950 to 6.5 billion in 2005, while the Catholic population grew from 459 million to 1.1 billion—meaning that both grew by a factor of roughly 2.5 times, so that the overall expansion of the Catholic Church roughly kept pace with the global population. That total, however, glosses over wide regional differences. The Church suffered serious losses in the North, but grew dramatically in the South.

The population of Latin America and the Caribbean went from just over 60 million in 1900 to 167 million in 1950, and to 561 million by 2000. The Catholic share of the Latin American population actually declined over this period, from 97 percent to just over 80 percent today, but the raw number of Catholics soared to 449 million. In Africa, the total population went from 224 million in 1950 to 905 million in 2000, and in Asia it grew from 1.4 billion in 1950 to 3.6 billion in 2000; and in both instances the Catholic share of the population outpaced overall growth. The total number of African and Asian Catholics grew enormously, to 130 million and 107 million respectively by the year 2000.

As lower global fertility levels begin to kick in worldwide during the twenty-first century, the Catholic population will probably begin to decline along with the overall population. This century will therefore likely not witness the same explosive Catholic growth as the last.

*2. Local Control.* In many parts of the global South, the number of Western missionaries peaked around Vatican II in the mid-1960s and then began to decline. In part, this drop-off was related to post–Vatican II declines in the priesthood and religious life; in part, it was the result of a conscious Catholic policy of encouraging local control of the Church, promoting indigenous vocations and leadership. This transition to local control, many experts believe, contributed to Catholic expansion.

Froehle observes that when a church is dependent largely upon foreign missionaries, most incentives cut against rapid growth. Foreign personnel and money are relatively fixed, so bringing in rising numbers of converts puts greater strains on a limited set of resources. When the church is locally run, on the other hand, growth can become self-sustaining, as personnel and resources expand with overall membership. To put this simplistically, 1 million new Nigerian Catholics can't produce a single new Irish missionary, but they can produce lots of Nigerian priests. The more a church is seen as local, the greater its potential for long-term growth.

Pentecostal writer Allan Anderson argues that one factor fueling the expansion of Pentecostalism in the twentieth century was its "church-planting" approach to evangelization, which meant the quickest possible transition to indigenous leadership. Moreover, Anderson says, many of the largest and most successful forms of Pentecostalism in the global South were unrelated to Western missionary efforts, such as the Akurinu movement in East Africa or the Indian Pentecostal Church of God. The late-twentieth-century expansion of Protestant Christianity in China likewise began during the Cultural Revolution, at a time when it was virtually impossible for foreigners to even set foot on Chinese soil, let alone direct missionary enterprises. These observations tend to confirm Froehle's argument, that homegrown Christianity is best positioned for rapid expansion.

*3. Local Circumstances.* Historical processes in Africa help explain why both Christianity and Islam prospered in the twentieth century. Though exact numbers are impossible, owing to imprecise and often politically skewed census methods, the best guess by most demographers is that there are close to 400 million Muslims and 400 million Christians in Africa today, each representing more than 40 percent of the total population. Jesuit Fr. Tom Michel, one of Catholicism's leading experts on Islam, has pointed out that Africa in the twentieth century was among the last places on earth where old tribal religions broke down, and the population chose from among the major faiths on offer, Islam and Christianity. The two achieved a rough stalemate, making them a bit like the Coke and Pepsi of global religion.

Similarly, Catholicism's gains in India reflect unique historical and social factors. Catholicism had its greatest missionary success among the Dalits, the permanent underclass of the Indian caste system, who often see choosing a non-Hindu religion as a means of rejecting oppression. Dalits account for somewhere between 60 and 75 percent of the total Catholic population of India. In South Korea, most experts believe that the dramatic expansion of Catholicism in the second half of the twentieth century is related in part to the leadership role played by Catholic activists in Korea's prodemocracy movement, especially Catholic layman Kim Dae-jung, who served as the country's president from 1998 to 2003 and who is known as the "Asian Mandela."

What these examples demonstrate is that no "one-size-fits-all" explanation for Catholic growth or decline is possible. In every part of the world, growth or decline is connected in part to local circumstances, and the future prospects for the Church will rise or fall as those circumstances evolve. For example, Catholicism could score significant missionary gains in China if the climate for religious liberty improves. There's already movement afoot; by one estimate, there are now substantially more Christians in China than Communists. (Roughly 50 million Chinese are formal party members, while best-guess estimates for all Chinese Christians, Protestants and Catholics together, is around 80 million.)

4. *Absorbing Indigenous Culture.* Gambian scholar Lamin Sanneh, a Catholic convert who teaches at Yale University, observes that Christianity had an important edge over Islam in some parts of Africa in its capacity to absorb the local language and culture, as opposed to Islam's need to "Arabize" its converts. This point too is counterintuitive, since critics have often accused Christianity of imposing European culture upon converts. To paraphrase von Clausewitz's famous remark about war, Christian evangelization has usually been seen as an extension of colonialism by other means.

In reality, Sanneh says, the explosion of Christianity was as much a reaction against colonialism as it was a product of it. Christianity, he found, grew where the local culture had preserved the indigenous name for God, as well as aspects of the native religion; Islam was successful where the indigenous religion had largely been obliterated. The capacity to "baptize" preexisting cultural traditions, and to insert them into a Christian context, has always been part of Christianity's missionary genius. The transition in Catholicism after Vatican II to celebrating Mass and the other sacraments in the local languages, according to experts such as Sanneh, was an enormous missionary asset in much of the global South. . . .

# Periodical Bibliography

*The following articles have been selected to supplement the diverse views presented in this chapter.*

Riazat Butt
and John Hopper — "Senior Catholic Warns Off Anglican Church's Women Priest Opponents," *Guardian*, November 20, 2009. www.guardian.co.uk.

Gianni Cardinale — "The Growth of Catholics in Africa," *30Days*, June/July 2006. www.30giorni.it.

Catholic News Agency — "Priest Shortage Stems from Crisis of Faith, Ignorance of the Infinite, Not Celibacy, Say Bishops," October 13, 2005. www.catholicnewsagency.com.

Laurie Goodstein — "Hispanics Reshaping U.S. Catholic Church," *New York Times*, April 25, 2007.

Kate Childs Graham — "Why I'm Not a Nun," *National Catholic Reporter*, March 26, 2009. http://ncronline.org.

Richard McBrien — "A Pastorally Sensible Solution to the Priest Shortage," *National Catholic Reporter*, January 26, 2009. http://ncronline.org.

Julie McCarthy — "Catholic Church Losing Ground in Latin America," NPR Online, May 12, 2007. www.npr.org.

Judith Shulevitz — "The Power of the Mustard Seed," *Slate*, May 12, 2005. www.slate.com.

John Thavis — "Vatican Stats Confirm Growth of Church, Especially in Asia, Africa," Catholic News Service, February 12, 2007. www.catholicnews.com.

Terry Wynn — "How Can Nuns Survive in America?" MSNBC, April 14, 2005. www.msnbc.com.

# For Further Discussion

## Chapter 1

1. Marc Pascal says that celibacy for priests is "without any meritorious religious basis." Does Cale Clark provide a meritorious religious basis for celibacy? Explain your reasoning.

2. Jennifer Ferrara argues that a priest is an icon of God as father, and therefore that women cannot be priests. How does John Wijngaards respond to this argument? Do you find his response persuasive? What arguments (if any) does Ferrara advance that Wijngaards does not answer?

## Chapter 2

1. After looking at the viewpoints by David France and Daniel Burke, does the case of Paul Shanley indicate that the Church's sex abuse scandal was linked to gay priests? Explain your reasoning.

2. Based on Rod Dreher's arguments, should gay men leave the Catholic Church? Explain your reasoning.

## Chapter 3

1. Anthony Stevens-Arroyo argues that Catholics should push for what kind of stem cell research? Do bishops appear to be following Stevens-Arroyo's advice, according to Nancy Frazier O'Brien?

2. Rich Deem argues that the Catholic Church is not responsible for the spread of AIDS because Catholics who choose to ignore the Church on celibacy are not likely to choose to obey the Church by refusing to use condoms. According to Marcella Alsan, why is focusing on the choice of celibacy and the choice of condom use in this issue misleading?

## Chapter 4

1. Does the viewpoint by Ruth Gledhill and her colleagues tend to support or refute Christopher Chantrill's claim that stricter churches tend to grow more quickly than liberal ones?

2. Based on the viewpoints by Gerald Floyd and John L. Allen Jr., which do you think will be more important in the future of the Catholic Church—the absorption of some Anglicans or the growth of the Church in Africa? Explain your reasoning.

# Organizations to Contact

*The editors have compiled the following list of organizations concerned with the issues debated in this book. The descriptions are derived from materials provided by the organizations. All have publications or information available for interested readers. The list was compiled on the date of publication of the present volume; the information provided here may change. Be aware that many organizations take several weeks or longer to respond to inquiries, so allow as much time as possible.*

**Anglican Communion Office**
St. Andrew's House, 16 Tavistock Crescent
London  W11 1AP
  England
44 (0) 20 7313 3900 • fax: 44 (0) 20 7313 3999
e-mail: aco@anglicancommunion.org
Web site: www.anglicancommunion.org

The Anglican Communion is a church made up of more than 80 million members worldwide. It includes forty-four regional and national member churches around the globe in 160 countries. The Anglican Communion has a long history of ecumenical dialogue with the Roman Catholic Church. The Anglican Communion Web site includes numerous resources, including the Anglican Communion News Service and *Anglican Episcopal World Magazine*. The Web site also includes numerous discussions of Catholic/Anglican affairs.

**Catholics for Choice**
1436 U Street NW, Suite 301, Washington, DC  20009-3997
(202) 986-6093 • fax: (202) 332-7995
e-mail: cfc@catholicsforchoice.org
Web site: www.catholicsforchoice.org

Catholics for Choice is an advocacy group for Catholics who support a woman's moral and legal right to follow her conscience in matters of sexuality, reproductive freedom, and reproductive health. It conducts education and advocacy work in the United States, Europe, and Latin America. Publications produced by Catholics for Choice include *Sex in the HIV/ AIDS Era* and *You Are Not Alone: Information for Catholic Women on the Abortion Decision*. The organization also produces *Conscience*, a quarterly magazine.

## Catholic Health Association (CHA)

1875 Eye Street NW, Suite 1000, Washington, DC   20006
(202) 296-3993
e-mail: servicecenter@chausa.org
Web site: www.chausa.org

The Catholic Health Association (CHA) is the largest group of nonprofit health care sponsors, systems, and facilities in the United States. Catholic health facilities and hospitals provide health care to patients of all ages, races, and religious beliefs. The CHA publishes the semimonthly newsletter *Catholic Health World*, the bimonthly professional journal *Health Progress*, and the quarterly newsletter *Health Care Ethics USA*. Many articles from these publications are available on the CHA Web site.

## DignityUSA

PO Box 376, Medford, MA   02155
(202) 861-0017 • fax: (781) 397-0584
e-mail: info@dignityusa.org
Web site: www.dignityusa.org

DignityUSA is a Catholic organization of gay, lesbian, bisexual, and transgender (GLBT) persons who worship together and advocate for increased GLBT rights within the official church and in American society. DignityUSA publishes a weekly electronic newsletter, *Breath of the Spirit*; a monthly newsletter called *Dateline*; and the membership quarterly *Quarterly Voice*.

## Leadership Conference of Women Religious

8808 Cameron Street, Silver Spring, MD   20910

(301) 588-4955 • fax: (301) 587-4575
e-mail: clartey@lcwr.org
Web site: www.lcwr.org

The Leadership Conference of Women Religious (LCWR) is the association of the female leaders of congregations of Catholic nuns and other religious groups in the United States. It represents 95 percent of the women religious in the United States. LCWR attempts to promote beneficial systemic change; study significant trends and issues within church and society; stand in solidarity with those who experience violence and oppression; and create and offer resource materials on religious leadership skills to members and the public. LCWR holds a yearly national assembly. Its publications include the *LCWR Newsletter*, the *LCWR Annual Report*, and the journal *LCWR Occasional Papers*.

## National Organization for Marriage (NOM)

20 Nassau Street, Suite 242, Princeton, NJ 08542
(609) 688-0450 • fax: (888) 894-3604
e-mail: contact@nationformarriage.org
Web site: www.nationformarriage.org

National Organization for Marriage (NOM) is a nonprofit organization dedicated to protecting marriage and the faith communities that sustain it. It is involved in organizing opposition to initiatives relating to same-sex marriage at the state level through advocacy and building databases of voters and donors. NOM also operates the NOM Education Fund, which provides information and research on protecting marriage and preventing same-sex marriage to clergy, scholars, and politicians, and the NOM Marriage PAC, which raises funds directly for state political races. The NOM Web site includes press releases and information pages such as "The Threat to Marriage" and "Why Marriage Matters."

## Pew Forum on Religion & Public Life

1615 L Street NW, Suite 700, Washington, DC 20036
(202) 419-4550 • fax: (202) 419-4559

Web site: http://pewforum.org

The Pew Forum on Religion & Public Life is a nonpartisan, non-advocacy organization that seeks to promote a deeper understanding of issues at the intersection of religion and public affairs. It pursues its mission by delivering timely, impartial information to national opinion leaders, including government officials and journalists, but does not take positions on policy debates. At its Web site there are many surveys and event transcripts such as "Does Obama Have a Problem Among Catholic Voters?" as well as publications such as *Special Report: The Same-Sex Marriage Debate*. The Pew Forum also offers both an e-mail newsletter and an RSS news feed.

### United States Conference of Catholic Bishops (USCCB)

3211 Fourth Street NE, Washington, DC   20017-1194
(202) 541-3000 • fax: (202) 541-3412
Web site: www.usccb.org

The United States Conference of Catholic Bishops (USCCB) is the official organization of the Catholic hierarchy in the United States. The purpose of the conference is to promote the programs and biblical interpretations of the Church and carry out education and advocacy on various social issues based on Church doctrine and guidance. Publications produced by the Conference of Catholic Bishops include *Cultural Diversity: Theological and Pastoral Reflections* and *Married Love and the Gift of Life*.

### Vatican

Papal Basilica of Saint Peter
fax: 39-06-698-85793
Web site: www.vatican.va

The Vatican is a city-state within the city of Rome, which serves as the administrative center of the Catholic Church. The Vatican Web site includes a vast store of publications and resources, including texts of the pope's official statements, news reports, the daily *Bulletin of the Holy See Press Office*, links to the Vatican library, information on World Youth Day, and more.

**Women Priests**

111A High Street, Rickmansworth, Herts   WD3 1AN
  United Kingdom
44-1923-779446
e-mail: sophie@womenpriests.org
Web site: www.womenpriests.org

Women Priests is an international organization that works to promote the ordination of women as priests in the Catholic Church. Women Priests uses its Web site and other resources to educate Catholics and the public about the ordination of women priests. The Web site includes numerous articles and publications including ancient documents, papal statements, and papers such as *Women Bishops? Views in the Roman Catholic Church, Official and Otherwise* and *Church's View of Sex the Root Cause of Its Troubles.*

# Bibliography of Books

John L. Allen Jr.    *The Future Church: How Ten Trends Are Revolutionizing the Catholic Church.* New York: Doubleday, 2009.

John L. Allen Jr.    *The Pope's Men: The Inside Story of How the Vatican Really Thinks.* New York: Doubleday, 2004.

John L. Allen Jr.    *The Rise of Benedict XVI: The Inside Story of How the Pope Was Elected and Where He Will Take the Catholic Church.* New York: Doubleday, 2005.

Angela Bonavoglia    *Good Catholic Girls: How Women Are Leading the Fight to Change the Church.* New York: HarperCollins, 2005.

Kenneth Briggs    *Double Crossed: Uncovering the Catholic Church's Betrayal of American Nuns.* New York: Doubleday, 2006.

Sara Butler    *The Catholic Priesthood and Women: A Guide to the Teaching of the Church.* Chicago: Hillenbrand Books, 2006.

James D. Davidson    *Catholicism in Motion: The Church in American Society.* Liguori, MO: Liguori/Triumph, 2005.

Jay P. Dolan    *In Search of an American Catholicism: A History of Religion and Culture in Tension.* New York: Oxford University Press, 2002.

| | |
|---|---|
| John Fialka | *Sisters: Catholic Nuns and the Making of America.* New York: St. Martin's Press, 2003. |
| Andrew M. Greeley | *Priests: A Calling in Crisis.* Chicago: University of Chicago Press, 2004. |
| Deborah Halter | *The Papal "No": The Vatican's Refusal to Ordain Women.* New York: Crossroad Publishing Company, 2004. |
| Mary Jo Iozzio, Mary M. Doyle Roche, and Elise M. Miranda, eds. | *Calling for Justice Throughout the World: Catholic Women Theologians on the HIV/AIDS Pandemic.* New York: Continuum, 2008. |
| Mary Ellen Lopata and Casimer Lopata | *Fortunate Families: Catholic Families with Lesbian Daughters and Gay Sons.* Victoria, British Columbia, Canada: Trafford Publishing, 2003. |
| Mary J. McDonough | *Can a Health Care Market Be Moral?: A Catholic Vision.* Washington, DC: Georgetown University Press, 2007. |
| Donald E. Messer | *Breaking the Conspiracy of Silence: Christian Churches and the Global AIDS Crisis.* Minneapolis, MN: Augsburg Fortress, 2004. |
| Dale O'Leary | *One Man, One Woman: A Catholic's Guide to Defending Marriage.* Manchester, NH: Sophia Institute Press, 2007. |
| John W. O'Malley | *What Happened at Vatican II.* Cambridge, MA: Harvard University Press, 2008. |

Leon J. Podles — *Sacrilege: Sexual Abuse in the Catholic Church*. Baltimore, MD: Crossland Press, 2007.

Joe Rigert — *An Irish Tragedy: How Sex Abuse by Irish Priests Helped Cripple the Catholic Church*. Baltimore, MD: Crossland Press, 2008.

Michael S. Rose — *Goodbye, Good Men: How Liberals Brought Corruption into the Catholic Church*. Washington, DC: Regnery Publishing, 2002.

Todd A. Salzman and Michael G. Lawler — *The Sexual Person: Toward a Renewed Catholic Anthropology*. Washington, DC: Georgetown University Press, 2008.

Moises Sandoval — *On the Move: A History of the Hispanic Church in the United States*. 2nd ed. Maryknoll, NY: Orbis Books, 2006.

Richard A. Schoenherr — *Goodbye Father: The Celibate Male Priesthood and the Future of the Catholic Church*. New York: Oxford University Press, 2002.

John Vidmar — *The Catholic Church Through the Ages: A History*. New York: Paulist Press, 2005.

# Index

# R

Racial discrimination, Church opposition to, 89, 120
Ranch, Jonathan, 110
Ratzinger, Cardinal Joseph
  comments on Islam, 15–16
  election to papacy, 14–15
  political philosophy condemnation, 15
  *See also* Benedict XVI (Pope)
"Real Love for Homosexuals" (Morrison), 102
Repression and the sex abuse scandal, 104–112
Rhythm method (of birth control), 123–124
Rich, Frank, 85
Rigali, Cardinal Justin, 134, 140–141
Right-wing opposition to gay priests, 64–65, 68
Ripley, Amanda, 61
Robinson, B. A., 61
Rock, Allan, 75
Roman Empire
  destruction of Christian communities, 55
  discrimination in, 47–48
Romans, Book of, 77

# S

Same-sex marriage. *See* Gay marriage
Scheidt, Daniel, 41–42
Schindler, David, 43
Scriptural teachings about homosexuality, 77–78
Second Vatican Council, 54–55, 66, 76

Self-giving concept, 36–37
Sexual abuse scandal, 64, 67
  economic costs to the Church, 114
  France's book about, 105
  gay priests as non-focus of, 113–117
  homophobia/repression and, 104–112
  John Jay College study, 114, 115
  Nienstedt's questioning of findings, 115–116
  Paul Shanley's role, 108–111
Sexual blackmail, 72
Sexual crisis in the Catholic Church, 41
Sexual intercourse/relations for procreation, 91–94
Sexuality
  exploitation/suppression of others via, 36, 84
  importance of honesty about, 65–66, 65–67
  view of John Paul II, 36–37
  *See also* Gay priests; Gays (homosexuals)
Sexuality in marriage, 127–132
  avoidance of sex, 129–131
  ignoring Church advice about, 130
  love and forgiveness, 131–132
  prayer before sex, 128–129
Shanley, Father John, 105
Shanley, Rev. Paul
  counseling service, 108
  NAMBLA participation, 110–111
  pedophilia charges against, 109